Forecasting Your School's Funding

Julie Cordiner & Nikola Flint

First published in Great Britain in 2019
by School Financial Success Publications
Copyright © 2019 Julie Cordiner & Nikola Flint

ISBN-13: 978-0995590229

To our families, especially the younger generations.

Inspiring School Financial Success to support schools today

for a brighter future tomorrow.

FOREWORD

Are you a mainstream headteacher, principal or school business leader, worried about your budget and wondering how the school funding reforms will affect your school in the future? How can you even start to plan ahead when there are so many uncertainties?

School financial leadership is essential to survive these challenging times. Strategic financial planning is an important part of this, as a means of achieving your vision, giving you confidence that you are in control of whatever funding you receive and are able to spend it well on the priorities that matter to you.

A vital mechanism for achieving robust financial planning is a multi-year budget plan, which sets out the expected cost of running the school in the medium-term. It anticipates changes in the curriculum, staffing, pupil numbers, and other aspects of how the school is run. This provides reassurance to your funding body that you have a sustainable budget and can fulfil your delegated responsibilities.

But one of the challenges of the English school funding system is that leaders are expected to plan ahead and manage very large budgets in a high-stakes accountability system, with virtually no information about how much money they might receive beyond the current year.

Your future funding is the missing piece of the forward planning jigsaw. Without it, how do you know your plans are affordable?

This book is very practical in nature: it provides a step-by-step toolkit that shows you how to create a high-level set of scenarios for your school's funding over a three-year period. You will then be able to use these scenarios as the basis for your three-year budget planning.

For maintained schools, this will provide excellent evidence of compliance with Section B of the School Financial Value Standard (SFVS), Setting the Budget. The support notes for the SFVS recommend the use of scenarios for your funding and expenditure.

For established academies, our advice will be a huge help in completing your three-year budget forecast return (BFR) each July. For new academies it will mean you can prepare a robust first In-Year Budget Return (IYBR) before you are required to complete the full BFR.

For all schools, the system we advocate will help you to achieve a meaningful three-year budget plan, instead of that 'tick in the box' feeling that emerges when financial forecasts feel like a stab in the dark. This is an analogy that we've heard from many SBLs in recent years, and it's time to change it.

Our approach will help you to stimulate a debate among your leadership team and governors, Trustees or members about how you would respond to changes in funding levels. These discussions are an essential part of your forward planning. They can be challenging, because they may bring out deeply-held beliefs and attitudes, sometimes exposing conflicting views about which priorities are most important for your school.

But it's essential to work through all of this if you are to achieve your vision within limited resources. The key is to know what funding you are likely to have and target it at the activities that are most important and most effective in securing improved outcomes for the children and young people in your care.

By following the steps that we've set out in this guide, you will be able to develop a strategy for responding to changes in funding, with the ultimate aim of achieving a sustainable financial position.

Having a strategy in mind that is sensitive to future changes in funding will enable you to exercise a measure of control over your situation, at a time when this might seem impossible. You will be able to refer to your strategy and take early action when opportunities present themselves, such as unexpected staff turnover and expiry of contracts for goods and services. This will lead to better decision-making which is rooted in your priorities and is in line with your vision and school development plan.

The content in 'Forecasting Your School's Funding' is intended to be accessible and flexible, providing guidance on how to construct your own model to achieve multi-year forecasts of your funding. This will enable you to apply your own preferences and style of presentation.

We also explain the benefits of scenario planning, emphasising the importance of setting expectations early on in the process, and we consider how to engage your senior leadership team and governors, trustees or members in the debate about the assumptions to be used in the model. The way in which you approach the exercise will influence its success.

Readers who have seen an advance copy of the book have highlighted the considerable benefits of constructing a model like this yourself. You can fully appreciate the significance of the decisions you make and can adapt the approach to suit your own circumstances or your level of certainty about different elements within the model. It will also make it easier to amend the forecasts as further information becomes available, and you will be able to roll the model forward in subsequent years.

Once you have arrived at your three scenarios and have used them to develop multi-year budget plans, we suggest an approach for presenting your work to various stakeholders in the form of a Financial Sustainability Plan. You can tailor the plan to reflect your own approach and findings.

As part of the process of guiding you through the construction of the scenarios, we will help you to understand the national funding reforms and consider the impact they could have on your financial position. This is a key element of some of the decisions you will take as you work through the model.

Blending this knowledge with your local intelligence about what might happen to pupil numbers in the coming years will enable you to create robust scenarios to support your multi-year budget plans. We will highlight the things you need to know about the funding reforms and suggest other issues to consider at the appropriate time, as we go through the steps of building the model.

Our other books, 'School Budget Mastery' and 'Leading a School Budget Review', deal with the next steps after you have fed the forecasts into your budget planning systems. The first of these books provides an overview and checklists for your budget preparation and review processes. The second shows you how to undertake a fundamental budget review so that you can balance the budget and achieve value for money. At the end of this book you will find a link to our website, where further details can be found about these publications.

CONTENTS

1 INTRODUCTION

Financial leadership

School leaders can make a huge difference to staff performance and pupil outcomes. The role is multi-dimensional and complex. Aspiring headteachers develop skills in most areas relating to teaching and learning and leadership of people as they rise through the ranks. Aspiring school business leaders will have a firm grasp of financial processes and controls and will have developed skills in staff management and possibly a wide range of non-finance areas.

However, in the past, preparation for these leadership posts has not always paid as much attention to strategic financial leadership. If you are a headteacher, think back to your experience. Did you receive sufficient training in the financial aspects of the role before being handed responsibility for a multi-million-pound budget? Many have told us that they didn't. Even with an excellent School Business Leader, you need a clear understanding of your own strategic role, as you are the one who will ultimately be held responsible if things go wrong.

This lack of attention to strategic financial leadership is quite surprising when you consider the scale of the budgetary challenges that have been faced by schools in recent years. The situation is somewhat better for those in the school business stream, especially now the creation of the Institute of School Business Leadership is providing a much stronger focus on the leadership aspects of the role.

In our first school funding guide, 'School Budget Mastery', we defined strategic financial leadership as 'creating a vision for how the available resources will be used to achieve your school's aims in the longer term and implementing that vision in a way that creates the conditions for sustainable improvement'.

The big question is, what will the 'available resources' look like in the future? Funding reforms have changed the landscape and made it much more difficult to predict how much money anyone will receive in future. Moreover, the last three years of unfunded pressures have led to rising numbers of schools spending above their income or falling into deficit.

Funding has become a vital issue for all school leaders. It has therefore become evident that a more strategic approach is needed in order to manage the situation. In a time of huge uncertainty, schools need to identify the things they do have some control over and take action to turn them to the school's advantage.

Leaders need to be in full control of their budget, while scanning the horizon for future changes that will impact on either the funding received or the need to spend. While the headteacher has the lead responsibility, a team effort is needed to achieve financial sustainability. This includes senior and middle leaders, the school business leader, budget holders (i.e. anyone who takes spending decisions) and governors. We will use the terms 'governor' and 'Governing Body' in this book as shorthand, to include trustees, members and the relevant governance structures in academies.

This book is designed to raise awareness of one particular aspect of financial leadership: strategic financial planning, which is an important technique for achieving a sustainable budget in these challenging times. By following our recommended approach, you can develop funding scenarios based on robust assumptions as a starting point for your multi-year budget.

The context for your financial planning

Schools are complex organisations with multiple layers of accountability, high expectations placed on leaders, and constant change imposed by the government. Because education is funded by the taxpayer, there is a lot of pressure to demonstrate value for money, which most people would agree is a reasonable requirement.

The problem is that the inadequate level of school funding has become a fundamental issue, with many more schools facing a financial crisis than before. The National Funding Formula (NFF) has been presented as a solution to the problem of some schools being underfunded, but in reality, it is simply a fairer distribution of not enough money.

While the government repeatedly insists there is more money in education than ever before, this is largely down to the fact that there are more pupils than ever before. The extra funding for growth in rolls does not address the fundamental shortfall between funding and actual costs. In fact, every extra pupil makes the gap worse.

The government says it is protecting funding in real terms compared to 2017/18 levels, but this baseline includes unfunded pressures which schools have had to absorb. These include increases in national insurance, pension contributions, inflation on goods and services, and in some cases the Apprenticeship Levy.

The Department for Education (DfE) itself estimated that schools would experience cumulative cost pressures of 3.4% in 2016/17, rising to 8.7% by 2019/20. No wonder schools are facing financial difficulties - a shortfall has been built into the system. Schools that are spending a higher than average proportion of their budget on staffing are likely to be experiencing the greatest difficulties, because this is where the unfunded pressures are.

What impact has this had? We can get a sense of it from the 2017/18 balances for LA schools, published in December 2018 at:

https://www.gov.uk/government/statistics/la-and-school-expenditure-2017-to-2018-financial-year.

Some of the most striking facts are:

- There was an increase in the percentage of all LA schools in deficit, from 9.1% in March 2017 to 10.2% in March 2018.
- The average mainstream school deficit rose by 16%, from £131k to £152k. The average surplus rose by 3.1%, from £131k to £135k.
- Sector results varied: the secondary school average deficit was £484k (16.3% higher than the previous year), compared to the average deficit of £50k for primary schools (up by 13.6%).
- The school-level file shows that overall, 6,703 out of 15,050 LA maintained schools (44.5%) spent more than their income in 2017/18. Broken down by sector, 56% of secondary schools and 43.7% of primary schools had an in-year deficit.

Figures are available for academies up to August 2017 at the time of writing, showing that 6.1% of trusts had a cumulative deficit (an increase of 0.6% from the previous year) and 2.3% had a zero balance. However, these statistics are not comparable with LA schools because they were only published at trust level, which is the legal entity. Some academies in deficit were not reflected in the report because their Multi Academy Trust (MAT) was in surplus overall. You can see the details at: https://www.gov.uk/government/statistics/academy-trusts-with-a-revenue-surplus-or-deficit-2016-to-2017.

These statistics suggest that the financial planning methods used in the past may not have provided sufficient advance warning of the looming gap between funding and expenditure. It also seems that many schools and academies have not responded promptly enough to the problems that have been building up as a result of insufficient funding to cover cost pressures over the last two to three years.

In this sort of situation, financial planning becomes critical if you are to stand any chance of achieving a sustainable budget.

There is also a tactical reason to improve. As long as the DfE can identify cases of financial mismanagement, waste, and the failure of schools to take action early enough to prevent deficits, it will be much more difficult for schools to argue that current levels of funding are insufficient and for the Secretary of State to make the case to the Treasury for more money in the Spending Review which determines the future funding available to education.

For some situations, a light-touch approach may have been sufficient in the past, when budgets were relatively stable. With so much uncertainty about the new school funding arrangements, there is a need for higher-level financial leadership skills to deal with the wide-ranging changes that lie ahead. We hope that our approach to strategic financial planning will help you in your journey.

Why is financial planning challenging?

The ESFA requires academies to submit three-year budgets by the end of July each year via the Budget Forecast Return (BFR). Many local authorities already have a provision in their local Scheme for Financing Schools for LA maintained schools to do the same.

Since these funding bodies are unable to provide robust multi-year funding information, you can appreciate the irony of this requirement. Nevertheless, financial planning for the medium term is an important technique to support strategic financial leadership and achieve a sustainable budget. If you haven't put much thought into how much money you are likely to receive in future, your attempt at a three-year plan is likely to be little more than aspirational guesswork.

The school's reserves strategy takes on an added importance when funding is insufficient to fully cover your ongoing costs. Academies are expected to work towards a reserves target of two months' worth of salaries, which seems a very steep challenge in the current climate.

Of course, reserves can only be used once, then they're gone. But with careful management, a school can use them to sustain current levels of staffing until full year savings can be achieved from a restructure.

When a school is growing organically (rather than adding entire classes or year groups), it has to absorb the cost of additional pupils who arrive in September. They won't attract funding until the start of the following financial year; this can be a whole year's delay for academies, unless they are funded on estimated pupil numbers.

On top of concerns about the overall quantum being insufficient, the National Funding Formula (NFF) introduced in April 2018 involves a redistribution of funding between schools in different parts of the country. The ability to predict the pace of transition to the pure formula is limited because of the complexities of the NFF and the continuing LA discretion over the local formula.

This discretion has now been extended by another year, to 2020/21, because DfE has observed that the majority of LAs moved towards the NFF in their decisions for 2018/19.

So far, the DfE has not disclosed when the 'Hard NFF' will be introduced; the earliest possible date is 2021/22. It will depend on when room becomes available in the parliamentary calendar for the primary legislation that it requires. DfE also needs to find solutions for items such as rates, PFI costs, and pupil mobility, which need to be brought into the national formula. These items have so far been funded on the basis of what each LA spent in the previous year; the government needs to standardise the process because it does not have the capacity to calculate specific costs like these for individual schools.

The timing of information hasn't changed with the advent of the NFF, because of the way in which the Treasury decides funding for government departments. The DfE has only been able to outline funding levels up to 2019/20, the year which marks the end of the current Spending Review period. The Education Select Committee inquiry into school and college funding is asking whether the fixed period is appropriate as a method for funding a core service such as education.

At present, a multi-year forecast of a school's future funding is therefore the missing piece of the financial planning jigsaw.

What are the risks in not planning ahead?

Some leaders will feel that there is little point in even trying to build predictions, due to all the uncertainties. They will say that they simply don't have the information on which to base their forecasts, so they will just try to ride it out and wait for more concrete information. Sometimes, governors won't challenge this theory because they are understandably uncomfortable with the prospect of restructuring and potential job losses.

The trouble with this line of thinking is that it doesn't take very long to send a school budget spiralling into deficit, but it can take a prolonged period of hard work and some very painful decisions in order to climb out of it, especially if you leave it too late.

We've seen examples of this in our own work. Julie supports schools and academies in financial difficulty as an education funding specialist and has carried out the local authority role in assessing licensed deficit applications and monitoring recovery plans. Nikola is a Specialist Leader of Education (SLE) and has undertaken financial reviews of schools to support overall school improvement programmes.

In many cases, schools that have fallen into deficit have not thought about how the NFF will affect them, mainly because they don't feel they have sufficient information to identify the potential impact. Often, they have also failed to monitor what's happening to their costs, especially as rolls change, and have not taken action quickly enough once a problem is spotted.

If a school or academy can't balance the budget, it's required to notify its funding body, who will swing into action to reduce the risk by applying their formal procedures.

A MAT will be expected to manage academy deficits within the trust. Unless there is a really solid culture of shared problems and mutual support, trustees could face disgruntled leaders from the other academies who are asked to give up reserves or pay an increased top slice to underwrite the shortfall while a recovery plan is implemented.

If a MAT or stand-alone academy goes into deficit or there are serious concerns about financial management, ESFA will issue a financial notice to improve. This usually results in the automatic withdrawal of delegation, removing any decision-making powers from the Trust or academy.

LAs will expect maintained schools to produce a recovery plan, usually to bring the budget into balance within three years. They can also issue warning notices and withdraw delegation if they don't have confidence in the school's recovery plan.

Whichever route you end up following, it's not a pleasant experience. In our view, it is far better for you, your staff and pupils to stay in control of your school's destiny and get things working in line with your original vision. It will still involve difficult decisions, but you will decide the approach and determine the pace of change.

How to get it right

There are many things you can't control in relation to your future financial position. It's best not to worry too much about these issues, and instead focus on what you <u>can</u> control, to put yourself in the best possible position.

Despite the uncertainties around future funding, it is still important to have in mind an over-arching financial strategy, so that you know what you are aiming for. The big picture is unlikely to change: your ultimate aim will be to achieve a sustainable budget that delivers your educational objectives. It's the smaller details that might vary, but you can adapt your plans to cope with those.

If you can understand your starting point and estimate the broad impact of funding reforms on your school, based on reasonable assumptions, you can do some early planning to identify how you would respond to any shortfall in funding over the next three years. It might be a rough estimate, but it's better than nothing, and can be tweaked as further information becomes available.

Without any sense of the level of funding available, how do leaders know that their budget plans are affordable? Any real terms reduction in grant could plunge the school into deficit, leading to urgent action being taken which may not be in the best interests of children or staff.

Earlier, we said that given all the uncertainties within the NFF, accuracy isn't achievable, but that this should not prevent you from trying to forecast your future funding as a basis for your three-year budget. We hope we've convinced you that in fact it's essential to make forecasts as a basis for sound debate and forward planning.

This book will show you how to produce a range of scenarios so that you can be prepared, no matter which direction your funding takes. The approach involves using whatever information is available to prepare broad-brush options for your future funding as the basis of a three-year budget plan.

If you scan the horizon and look for clues, there are often indications of changes which you can use to make an informed set of assumptions about how your funding might change in the next couple of years. The important thing then is to act on it.

Before embarking on the model, let's take a look at some of the key issues that you will want to build into your forecasting.

Important issues to consider

Pupil numbers and characteristics

We've been through a period of sustained growth in population, which has now worked through to the secondary sector. However, we are now seeing a change in patterns between the sectors.

In some areas, primary schools are now feeling the effects of the birth rate levelling out, and rolls are declining in some cases, as competition for pupils becomes more intense.

In the secondary sector, LAs are working with schools and academies to meet demand for new places. There could be competition from new and expanding schools locally, or pupils could make different choices based on the various curriculum offers in the local area. Admissions in all types of school can be affected by Ofsted judgements.

With the current trend of a higher proportion of funding being allocated on pure pupil numbers, it doesn't necessarily require a big change in rolls for a school to feel a significant impact on its funding.

It's worth keeping your eye on the local authority's pupil number projections and being aware of parental views and the existence of any pre-school siblings in your pupils' families, so that you are wise to the potential for variations in admissions patterns before they occur.

Similarly, changes in pupil and school characteristics could cause a reduction in your funding. For example, free school meal (FSM) eligibility is a significant element for many schools; if you are not assiduous in getting parents to apply, you could see an adverse impact on your budget share or GAG.

The NFF now allows the use of both single census and Ever 6 FSM factors in the school funding formula, where previously an LA had to choose one of them. The balance between the two factors and the values attached to them could affect you. Making sure your data is correct in every respect is absolutely crucial.

Sometimes you might see a reduction in funding even if your rolls and characteristics have stayed the same. This could occur where a local authority is finding it difficult to balance the formula to the available funding. It may decide to allocate the same amount of money to a particular factor as in the year before, even if the data has increased. This will spread the money more thinly, reducing the unit value.

If your data is static but other schools in your area have a higher number of qualifying pupils, yours will be a smaller proportion of the total data and you could receive a reduced allocation. When we move to the Hard NFF, your data will be measured against national data.

LA formula decisions

Deliberate changes in the local formula can also have an impact. Your local authority will still control the distribution of funding locally up to and including 2020/21, choosing whether to adopt the NFF values fully or partially, or to stay with their existing formula. As we go through the modelling process, we will explain the impact of these decisions and show you how you can use this knowledge to make robust assumptions about your future level of per-pupil funding.

While it's obviously vital to recognise the potential for your funding to reduce, for some schools the NFF can provide better levels of funding. You need to strike a balance between prudence and pessimism, which isn't easy in the current climate. Bear in mind that if you do see an increase in your per-pupil funding, the first call on it is likely to be to cover the cost pressures that all schools are facing. The pay grant may not cover your plans for the September 2018 pay award, as a recent example.

If you are too pessimistic, you might make unnecessary cuts to staffing or optional extras that benefit under-achieving groups. By the time you find out you have more funding than expected, it may be too late to undo these actions. The balance between the number on roll, pupil characteristics and the impact of the NFF is key to understanding where you should pitch your forecasts. Don't worry - our approach takes all of this into account and we'll explain it as we lead you through the process of building your model.

Organisational structures and staff deployment

Over the last year, we've spoken to many school business leaders and governors at network meetings and conferences about their struggles to achieve a balanced budget.

It's not surprising that the most significant concern relates to staffing, where changes take time to achieve, and require substantial consultation if major restructures are required.

There are many dimensions to the decisions that leaders need to take: changing the number of staff, the way in which they are deployed, questions over pay and conditions where academies have freedoms, and layers of leadership and management. With teacher retention and recruitment also being problematic, uncertainty over funding only compounds the difficulties.

The table below from the published November 2017 workforce census shows the number of staff in schools in England (in thousands). There has been a steady rise in the totals from 2011 to 2016, with a dip in 2017. There is an interesting change in the balance between teachers and teaching assistants over time.

Figure 1: Composition of the school workforce (FTE):

	Teachers		of which: teachers without QTS[1]		Teaching Assistants		School Support staff		Total FTE
	Number	%	Number	%	Number	%	Number	%	
2011	440.0	50.1	16.1	1.8	219.8	25.0	218.1	24.8	877.9
2012	445.4	49.4	16.0	1.8	232.3	25.7	224.7	24.9	902.4
2013	449.7	48.9	16.6	1.8	243.7	26.5	226.9	24.7	920.3
2014	454.9	48.3	20.3	2.2	255.1	27.1	232.0	24.6	942.0
2015	456.9	47.7	22.5	2.3	263.0	27.5	238.0	24.8	957.8
2016	457.2	47.7	22.2	2.3	265.6	27.7	235.0	24.5	957.8
2017	451.9	47.7	21.0	2.2	262.8	27.8	232.4	24.5	947.1

1. Qualified teacher status

Source: School Workforce Census 2011 – 2017

The steady increase in staffing up to 2015/16 set the baseline for a much higher cost in pay awards, incremental drift, threshold progression and on-costs. It has created a situation in many schools where the scope for savings outside of the pay budget is now very small. You will be well aware that it can take an awfully long time to achieve full year savings on salaries, because of notice periods and the need for salary safeguarding.

No-one came into the profession to make people redundant, but this can become a harsh reality when things have got so bad that staffing reductions are the only way to get back on track.

One of the hardest things to do is persuade governors to support a decision to cut jobs, so you need to be absolutely sure that this approach is necessary to secure the school's future financial health. Make sure you are deploying staff in the most efficient way, while having regard to workload and their health. Using Integrated Curriculum-led Financial Planning (ICFP) is a strategy used successfully in many schools and academy trusts and is recommended by DfE.

Some of you might have benefited from the reforms. If this is the case, we urge you not to fall into the trap of thinking that everything will be fine. Your local authority might take different decisions in future years (while they can still operate a local formula). Even schools gaining from the NFF might find the extra funding is not enough to cover rising costs, given the level of unfunded pressures already discussed. A change in rolls can quickly make the position worse.

Everything is relative to your local situation, and there will always be some unquantifiable pressures. Recent issues have included the late notification of recommendations for the teachers' pay award from September 2018 and the increase in employer contributions for the Teacher Pension Scheme (which has been delayed to September 2019). While funding is being made available, the formulaic approach for the pay grant is leading to winners and losers, and at the time of writing, the exact details of how the DfE will support the pension increase are unknown. There is no long-term guarantee for these grants.

Moving forward

There are so many aspects to consider when trying to achieve a sustainable budget. You are likely to be absorbed in your own school's difficulties, so it can be hard to take a helicopter view and spot the key issues that need to be addressed.

With hindsight, it's usually easy to see how problems have arisen; but prevention is far better than cure. We have therefore developed a a method to help you make forecasts of your future funding, based on robust assumptions, as a starting point for your journey towards a sustainable budget.

Once you have worked up your forecasts and assessed the savings you need to make, our book 'Leading a School Budget Review' provides a logical system with easy to follow steps and templates to help assess your position and take action on areas of your budget. It will also provide proof to governors that you have looked at every area of your budget before recommending any staffing changes.

How to use the book

Our approach to solve the problem of uncertainty over funding is based on scenario planning. This technique allows you to build a range of potential funding forecasts for the next three years.

We will cover the many benefits to this approach in Chapter 2, but above all it will raise awareness of the range of possibilities for your future funding and stimulate a debate about how you would respond to each of them. You will be better prepared, and it will make you feel able to exercise a degree of control over your situation, rather than be a victim of uncertainty.

By following our guidance, you will develop a set of forecasts to feed into your budget planning systems. You will also construct a Financial Sustainability Plan, which is a helpful tool in achieving engagement and building a team ethos to tackle the financial challenges you are facing. It can also be used to provide evidence to your funding body and other stakeholders that you have a robust strategy to deal with any future financial challenges.

Our method is based on a range of focused exercises which you can do for your own school, following our step by step instructions. In some cases, these activities may be best carried out by specific members of staff, but it will be important for the results to be discussed more widely across the leadership team and with governors. That way you will build a common purpose and shared responsibility for the actions that are needed to secure a sustainable budget.

However, it's vital that you allow sufficient time and support for the person who is completing the model to carry out the work, and that you check each stage together to make sure the assumptions are valid and consistent and that the results make sense. If new information becomes available, it will be easy to change it, but this should be by agreement.

How you use this book is up to you. One approach is to read through the narrative to learn what you need to do, and then develop your own approach to forecasting your funding.

But to get the full benefit, you can use the blend of information, tips and exercises that we have provided, and follow our end-to-end process for strategic financial planning and budget preparation. This approach culminates in the compilation of a Financial Sustainability Plan (FSP) in a format suitable for reporting to governors.

Your FSP will outline the funding scenarios and multi-year budget plans which you have produced and will recommend actions to ensure a balanced and sustainable budget, based on your school improvement and curriculum plans. It provides a sound strategic approach, founded on your educational vision for the school.

In some chapters we have provided web links to help you identify helpful information. These are correct at the time of writing, but we cannot guarantee that they will remain so. We will later mention a PDF which includes the hyperlinks for the web pages we quote.

Our model can be extended to roll forward the forecasts in future years, but you will need to check whether there are any changes in the way the NFF operates in future years, as this may affect your assumptions, or it could mean you need to make slight changes in the way the model works.

Throughout the book, we have used this icon to indicate an activity:

The end of the activity will be marked with a line of asterisks:

******

We recommend that you read through the book first, to gain an overview of the whole process. Then go back to each activity and consider which member of staff in your school is best placed to tackle it. They will suit different skills; some are objective, mathematical and technical, though they should be within the grasp of someone with fairly routine numeracy skills. Others need a more subjective approach.

As you go through the activities, you will be building up a portfolio of evidence, assumptions and findings, then devising solutions for whatever issues emerge.

Regardless of who is selected to carry out each activity, it is important to arrange planning time as a team to test the assumptions, confirm the conclusions and discuss what the results mean for your school. This is important professional development as well as being crucially important in achieving a common understanding of the challenges and ownership of the solutions.

Please note that throughout the book, references to headteachers and schools should be taken to include principals and academies. We will make clear any references that appertain to one type of school only, but fundamentally the approach to forecasting your future funding is the same, regardless of your legal status.

Are you ready to embark upon the journey to achieve school financial success through a sustainable budget? Then let's make a start.

2 THE SOLUTION: SCENARIO PLANNING

What is scenario planning?

We've already established that in the absence of any meaningful information about your future funding, it's best to develop your own method for making forecasts. This might sound ambitious, but as long as you devise a set of robust assumptions, it is possible to put together some reasonable estimates that you can justify.

There will inevitably be a margin of error in any forecasting, so we advocate scenario planning, which recognises that the future is uncertain.

Scenario planning is a helpful and flexible tool for presenting options that might happen in the future, in order to stimulate debate about how an organisation would respond in different situations.

We are proposing it as a way of producing high-level forecasts of your future funding, in order to support medium-term financial planning. It will help you to identify a range of possible outcomes and start thinking about how you would respond to each of them.

It means you will have a set of options (we recommend three) to consider as a first step, before you develop your three-year budget plans. You will be able to see the potential for different amounts of funding coming to your school over the period in question. This can deepen your thinking and open your eyes to the possibilities.

By comparing these funding scenarios with your current levels of expenditure, it will identify either the level of savings needed to achieve a balanced budget over the next three years, or the extra funding that you will have available to meet cost pressures and/or deal with the impact of rising rolls, whichever is relevant to your situation. Either way, it will help you to decide on the most efficient and effective deployment of the available funding and will guide you in developing a plan to achieve a balanced budget.

For multi-academy trusts, we suggest it's better to develop a set of scenarios for each individual academy. Their circumstances will be different, and the mix of rolls and funding will vary. If you practice pooling of GAG, you will want to aggregate the individual figures for each scenario at trust level, then realign them to each academy in line with your priorities.

This process may spark new ideas about how the trust's overall funding might change. It could also influence your priorities for investment in relation to supporting specific academies or trust-wide improvement.

Whatever your type of school, the process by which you develop your scenarios is just as important as the outcome of the exercise. Sharing ideas about your assumptions with fellow leaders and governors will open up discussions about the school's future ways of working. You will all develop a better understanding of the circumstances that affect your funding the most and you will see how even small changes in rolls or the structure of the local funding formula can have a disproportionate impact on your funding levels.

When you get to the stage of comparing your scenarios with your current expenditure, you will need to consider how you would respond if any of the three different levels of funding became a reality. As you go through this part of the process, you will need to think more strategically about what your priorities are.

Which areas do you value the most and would therefore want to preserve at all costs? Turn that round - are these 'non-negotiables' really essential? Are there some activities that you have always done without being sure they are effective? Would it be so bad to stop them?

You may experience some fascinating debates during this process, which reveal different values, attitudes and beliefs among your colleagues. It can produce some really strong discussions and challenges, and by tackling these together carefully, thoughtfully and with mutual respect, you can strengthen your leadership team and governing body, and the relationship between them.

Managing expectations

If you want to avoid any misunderstandings and, above all else, manage expectations, it is advisable to explain the principles of scenario planning before you start to engage staff, governors and any other stakeholders in it.

The first and most essential message is that the exercise is not guaranteed to provide an accurate prediction of your future funding. It is a broad brush set of multiple possibilities to use as a starting point for debating how the school would respond if faced with different levels of funding.

Everyone needs to understand that it is not possible to know what will happen beyond March 2020 at a national level, because the Treasury has not decided how much funding it will allocate for education. Until direct funding by the DfE is introduced, there will also be local variations. This will be crucial in gaining acceptance of the margin of error that exists when you are trying to make forecasts.

Scenario planning involves producing a range of high-level estimates based on a set of assumptions which may or may not materialise. It is not a detailed calculation of every element of your funding. You will be making assumptions for the main categories of grants, in order to produce best-case, middle-case and worst-case scenarios.

As we will see, there are various ways of arriving at these three estimates; choosing your final three will be a matter of judgement. This is no different to your usual practice in making assumptions about the expenditure and self-generated income elements of your three-year forward plan.

Your assumptions may need to change as decisions are taken by other parties, notably the DfE and your local authority. Even when LAs are no longer responsible for distributing school funding via a local formula, there will be areas of funding which they will still govern, particularly early years and high needs.

As more information becomes available, changes may need to be made to the assumptions on which the scenarios are based. Revisiting them at regular intervals will help to ensure that your plans are still on track.

Everyone involved in discussing the scenarios also needs to take responsibility for understanding and challenging the assumptions you have made. If any of these are patently unrealistic because they are either wildly optimistic or pessimistic, or if they rely on an unlikely combination of events, it would be unwise to base decisions on them.

There is a huge temptation to make the results fit what you would like the scenarios to be. We strongly advise you to resist this idea. Let the results speak for themselves, once you have made an honest assessment of the likely change in your per-pupil funding and rolls. It may be an eye-opener.

What are the benefits of scenario planning?

We advocate a scenario-based approach because it has many benefits that are applicable to schools in challenging financial circumstances.

Benefit 1: Demonstrating financial sustainability

The first benefit of scenario planning is a pragmatic one: it fulfils the expectations of your funding body that you will manage your delegated funding responsibly and prepare robust multi-year budget projections to prove that the school is financially secure.

Planning for only one year at a time is not a helpful practice; it engenders a feeling of being out of control. Your funding body needs to know that you are not going to plunge into deficit suddenly, and that you have a strategic plan to manage any changes in funding or spending requirements. They have written various conditions to achieve this reassurance into the relevant documents that govern your relationship with them: the LA Scheme for Financing Schools for LA maintained schools, and the Funding Agreement and Academy Financial Handbook for academies and free schools.

Demonstrating that you have gone through a proper process is key to building confidence in your ability to create and maintain a strategic plan. Scenario planning provides that proper process. It is completed by recording the stages you've gone through to get to the point where three scenarios for your future funding can be transferred into your budget planning software. You can present the results of your work in a Financial Sustainability Plan.

When we talk about building confidence, we don't only mean in relation to your funding body. The process also helps staff, governors and any other key stakeholders to know that you have a plan in place to handle any future changes in your circumstances. At a time when teacher retention is so important, you need to avoid any nervousness among staff as to whether their jobs are at risk due to a failure to plan ahead properly.

Our method will show you how to use the information that's available in order to make high-level forecasts of the key components of your funding. As more information emerges, you will be able to tweak your forecasts to take further steps towards the most likely and realistic scenario.

Benefit 2: Highlighting uncertainties in future funding

Expectations on school leaders are high. Staff will be looking to you for guidance and reassurance about their future employment and the direction in which the school is going. They may think that you have all the answers, and the weight of that expectation can be heavy.

But it simply isn't possible to predict anything in detail, as we've already demonstrated. Preparing several scenarios removes some of the tension from the task of producing an estimate of funding to enter into the school's multi-year budget plans. It helps you explain to those around you that you can't be expected to be precise about your future funding when there are so many things you can't control.

If you are an established academy, you will have completed your first attempt at the compulsory three-year budget return in July 2018. Many LA schools will also have been asked to do a similar exercise.

How was the experience? Did you find it easy to make assumptions on which to base your projections? Was it a case of guessing the percentage change in your GAG or budget share? How did you decide what pupil numbers were likely to materialise in the second and third year of your forecast? When ESFA reviews an academy's recovery plan, or when LA finance officers scrutinise budget plans or monitor schools with licensed deficits, there will be a lot of attention paid to the robustness of roll predictions.

Scenario planning encourages you to deal with the uncertainties by pulling apart the different components of your funding and examining how they could change. Understanding the impact of different options for rolls, pupil characteristics, the local formula and other grants provides an insight into the sensitivity of your funding.

This approach will expose areas where you are more reliant on particular funding streams, such as deprivation, low prior attainment, or SEN funding from the local authority's High Needs Budget. If your LA is moving towards the NFF, changes in the values for these factors could affect you.

If you are a relatively small school and the lump sum represents a higher proportion of your funding than it would for a large school, you will become more aware of any differences between the real cost of every additional pupil and the funding coming in for them.

Many of the changes are outside of your control, so they are difficult to predict. But it's important to identify those that you can influence, such as reviewing your curriculum offer, or improving parental perceptions by working with the LA's press office or the local press and radio stations to find ways of getting good news stories into local media in a targeted way.

Scenario planning is done at a high level, removing the expectation of accuracy. This can bring a sense of freedom and relief.

Benefit 3: Opening up debate

One of the most valuable benefits of scenario planning is that you can create the opportunity to stimulate a real debate about how the school would respond if the amount of money changed significantly, either for better or for worse.

Our terminology is deliberate. Yes, this is pretty much a marriage between you and your school's money. It's like any relationship - you may need to have discussions that you might previously have found hard to address. Perhaps you have actively avoided them because it all feels too difficult and potentially conflict-laden.

To achieve realistic scenarios, you need to form assumptions about the different elements of your funding. You need to be honest about whether you are being overly optimistic or pessimistic, and whether you even have a realistic option on the table as a result of your choices.

This will produce some interesting debates, such as people's beliefs about why parents decide to apply for a place at your school or not. It could also bring out some useful information that you might not be aware of, such as other schools' plans for expansion that governors are aware of through being a parent or grandparent. They might not have realised it was of interest to you.

Everyone will have a different perspective on what their school does with its money. Many people will hold views that are more to do with speculation than hard information, since it's not appropriate for everyone in a school to know everything about your finances. You are bound to get a wide range of views when you start talking about potential outcomes for your future budgets, whether that's at a very high level for a wider audience, or at a detailed level with individual budget holders.

This is where cultural issues can come to the fore. What is your attitude to money? Is it different from the attitude of the rest of your leadership team, or the governors on the Governing Board and Finance Committee? Are some of your staff or governors averse to planning, preferring to take a more laissez-faire approach? Getting a consensus can be tricky if there are a lot of subjective views on the topic of money.

When the whole of your Senior Leadership Team (SLT) and all governors can see the options for the school's future funding and have to think about how they would respond to them, it should open up a debate that focuses attention on the things that matter. It is human nature to keep doing things because we've always done them, because we like to stay within our comfort zone. But true learning happens outside your comfort zone.

If things which are regarded as important are placed under threat, people start to think much more creatively about how to preserve them. The debate can expose differences in opinion, and some leaders or governors may challenge whether a particular practice is still relevant or effective. This is healthy, because it gets to the heart of value for money considerations.

Even small changes can make a big difference to your success, when layered one on top of another. We only have to look at the approach taken by the British cycling team to understand this, where over time they focused on minute technical, psychological and physical details, all building together to ensure a perfect performance. There's no reason why a similar change management approach can't be applied in schools.

When making changes, the art is in handling challenge appropriately, discouraging colleagues from taking a defensive stance by opening up the discussion with careful questioning, allowing everyone to have their say until a consensus can be reached.

The process can encourage a collaborative approach. Starting early with a high-level analysis creates time and space to stimulate creative thinking. Take the opportunity to involve the whole school in considering different ways of working to achieve the changes that are necessary. This could include time-saving ideas, cost reductions, fund-raising ventures or relationships with local businesses or community organisations that bring benefits, either monetary or in-kind. You're not the only one who can have bright ideas!

Benefit 4: Quick wins

The final stage of building your scenarios will be the production of a Financial Sustainability Plan, which identifies the responses needed to the least likely scenarios and further develops the most likely one (usually your middle-case scenario) for detailed actions.

This is not a plan to be put on the shelf and forgotten about. You will want to update it whenever new information becomes available; the last thing you want to do is implement unnecessary savings, realising too late that a particular grant was available, or that pupil numbers were much better than expected.

The beauty of having a plan is that as opportunities present themselves, such as turnover of staff or expiry of contracts for goods and services, you will already know what you need to do. You have a plan to follow and can adopt the course of action you've already set, instead of starting from scratch. It's simply a matter of consulting your plan, taking the action and updating the plan to reflect the impact.

We call this the quick win benefit of scenario planning. You won't have to go through a fundamental decision-making process each time your circumstances change.

This will allow you to take advantage of a situation to secure early savings, which could make your financial position more secure and perhaps even prevent compulsory redundancies at a later stage. That will save you a lot of time, not to mention relief when you can avoid the emotional impact of causing someone to lose their job or seeing your staff go through a difficult process.

Benefit 5: Supporting continuous improvement

Scenario planning prompts you to re-examine your vision and priorities, as you identify different possibilities for your future funding. This is an invaluable process that will support your ongoing school development plan (SDP) and help you to achieve continuous improvement. Has the school development plan been subject to changes at regular intervals, or has it rolled on much the same for several years?

We've all heard the adage 'if you do what you've always done, you get what you've always got'. However, when everything around you is changing, continuing the same approach without re-assessing its effectiveness might actually result in worse outcomes.

As you record your findings from the exercises, you will naturally want to review whether your curriculum and staffing plans are still in alignment with your SDP and budget, another key element of strategic planning. Have both your data and the level of funding available been at the heart of your discussions?

It is easy to get caught up in exciting initiatives which you hope will transform outcomes for your pupils. But they need to be rooted in reality, otherwise you could end up spending money you haven't got, possibly on actions that don't actually secure improvement. You might appear to be efficient, but you could be doing the wrong things incredibly well. That won't help you achieve your vision.

Benefit 6: Creating a meaningful plan of action

Putting effort into identifying your scenarios and stating the assumptions that underpin them is a strategic exercise, but it has a real purpose in a pragmatic sense. It helps you to consider the impact of different levels of funding and to decide how you would respond to each of them. Your plans become a working document which is referred to and updated on a regular basis as more information becomes available.

This is all much more meaningful than a 'finger in the wind' exercise, which can feel like ticking boxes for the sake of it. You are choosing to examine your future financial position proactively and professionally, rather than producing a rough three-year plan because someone else has told you to do it.

A plan that is done grudgingly is likely to be submitted then shelved for another year because it isn't owned. Your plan, on the other hand, will be the outcome of deep thought and collaborative work with your key stakeholders, a blueprint for your future financial success.

How scenario planning works

We recommend the use of best, middle and worst-case scenarios for your future funding.

The worst-case scenario is your doomsday version, the least possible funding you might receive in the next three years. For schools that are not likely to see big gains from the NFF, we suggest using the Minimum Funding Guarantee percentage change, which is set out in the regulations governing school funding (more on this later). You hope that this scenario won't happen, but you need to allow for it being a possibility and be ready with plans for it. Given the levels of uncertainty, this is a prudent approach.

The best-case scenario is an optimistic one which you know is probably not going to happen, but it will allow you to be ambitious and forward-thinking. How might you use any additional funding to secure better outcomes or to better manage cost pressures? Or if you know the NFF is detrimental to your finances, what is the least poor option?

The middle-case scenario is probably going to be the most realistic one. It will reflect your local knowledge of what might happen with your local authority's decisions on the formula and how your pupil numbers are likely to change over the next three years.

Scenario planning isn't a technique where you fix figures and leave them alone. You can tweak different aspects of the model as further information becomes available. We have designed our method so that this is easy to do, with a minimum of input. Once your model has been created, you will enter information once but use it many times.

The model includes all types of funding. It doesn't include income that you generate yourself, as that will be netted off against your expenditure in your budget plans.

What are the key elements?

Thinking about the school funding system at the highest level, there are two main elements which when combined, drive your funding: the level of funding per pupil that you receive and the number of children on roll. For a high-level, broad-brush approach, we don't need to make it any more complicated than this.

First of all, you will identify your best, middle and worst case **per-pupil funding** by taking your baseline position and estimating how it will change over the three-year period under each option, using your local knowledge.

Next you will consider how your **rolls** could change, using a range of possibilities to construct best, middle and worst-case rolls over the same period.

Now for the interesting stage - you will combine all of these options by multiplying them against each other, as you can see below:

	Best £ per pupil	Middle £ per pupil	Worst £ per pupil
Best roll	1	4	7
Middle roll	2	5	8
Worst roll	3	6	9

This gives you nine options - but don't worry, we won't be asking you to develop nine budgets! You will choose the three most appropriate options as your final best, middle and worst-case scenarios. As you will see later, the process of deciding which three to choose can be a valuable exercise in itself.

Once you have established your three final scenarios from the nine, you can consider other sources of funding. These might include Pupil Premium, nursery allocations, post 16 funding, SEN funding and other grants. Once those are added in, you will have a range of three complete forecasts to transfer into your budget planning systems. You can then start to test out the implications of each one, identifying any shortfall against your current spending plans.

Limitations

There are limitations to this technique, and it's best to be aware of them before you embark upon it. Like any other system, it is only as good as the information that you put into it.

It will soon become clear that the assumptions you make about how your per-pupil funding and rolls will change in each scenario over the three-year period are critical to the results of this approach.

In fact, while this could be described as a limitation, there is great value in considering and agreeing the assumptions that you are building into the model. As we discussed earlier, simply opening up the discussion about them can identify in-built attitudes and values. A well-managed healthy debate will clarify things to everyone involved and provide a solid platform for agreement on the actions that are needed to set your budget in the right direction.

Given that the success of scenario planning hinges on the robustness of these assumptions, here are some suggestions to bear in mind as you go through the process:

- be clear about the assumptions that you need to make
- test them out with relevant colleagues
- consider what the margins of error might be and how they would impact on your forecasts and resulting actions
- keep the assumptions under review as you go through the process

As we guide you through the forecasting process, we will highlight issues that might influence the assumptions you make.

Fostering the right culture

The attitude towards money in your school can strongly influence your ability to set and achieve a sustainable budget. You can probably think of evidence to support this statement from your own experience; it can sometimes be difficult to persuade someone that a course of action is needed, if it runs counter to their own instincts and beliefs.

In the second of our school funding guides, 'Leading a School Budget Review', we discussed the importance of culture and how to build engagement with all staff, governors and other stakeholders to support your endeavours in balancing the budget.

This advice applies equally to the process of forecasting your future funding. You will need to involve a wide range of people in building your assumptions. It's worth remembering that as the person initiating the forecasts, you are some way ahead of everyone else in your thinking. Others need time to absorb the information and make sense of it before they can understand what you are trying to achieve, form a view on it and be willing to play a part. So you should think about how and when to communicate your progress and involve others.

The results will determine the actions that you take to bring the budget into balance over the next three years. They will have an impact on individuals. How will your staff and governors be affected by any changes that might need to be introduced? It's better for them to be involved in the process from an early stage, then they won't need time to catch up later on.

In 'Leading a School Budget Review', we talked about the 'Why, How, What' approach: **Why** the change is needed, **How** you plan to achieve it, and **What** you expect from everyone to ensure success.

By going through the process of identifying, testing and refining your assumptions to see how different sources of funding might change over the three-year period, you will build an awareness of how sensitive your funding is to different circumstances.

Sharing this process with staff and governors will help them to appreciate the different ways in which your financial position might develop in a relatively short period of time. This can be a bit of a revelation to some people, who shy away from thinking too far ahead when managing their own money, and who sometimes get into great difficulties as a result.

In producing a range of different funding options, you have an opportunity to engage more people in the debate about how you would respond to future shortfalls in funding. Allowing a reasonable amount of time for this exercise will help to build confidence and stimulate creative thinking, which is much better than a rushed set of decisions.

By creating a culture of openness and transparency, and valuing everyone's opinions, you can encourage people to offer their thoughts and jointly develop practical solutions. Often those who are carrying out tasks on a daily basis have a far better understanding of the potential for doing things differently and more efficiently.

We take a more in-depth look at how to generate the right sort of culture to address problem areas and get everyone on board in our book 'Leading a School Budget Review'. It contains some practical tips which you will be able to adapt to your scenario planning and the development of your Financial Sustainability Plan.

3 BUILDING THE FORECASTING MODEL

Overview of the model

This is not just a book; it's a practical toolkit which you can follow in order to produce three scenarios for your future funding as the basis of your three-year budget plan. In this chapter, we will explain the basic elements of the model, the information you need to make a start, and the ways in which you can tailor the model to suit your own preferences. We will also share some tips on how to build it.

On the face of it, the task of forecasting funding is relatively straightforward if we reduce it to the key components of the school funding system. As we said earlier, these are the average amount you receive per pupil and how many pupils you have.

There are lots of complications in the school funding system if you go more deeply into it. However, the purpose of your forecast is to raise awareness of the scope for changes in your funding, to stimulate debate and provide a basis for your strategic planning. So, let's keep it as simple as possible.

The reason for this level of simplicity will become clear as we start to develop the model. It quite quickly becomes multi-dimensional, because you will not only be considering three different options for each of the two elements, but also forecasting them over a period of three years.

We have adopted a terminology that distinguishes between the early development of **options**, combining best, middle and worst-case estimates of per-pupil funding and rolls (nine possibilities), and the resulting nine **scenarios**, from which you will choose three **final scenarios** to develop further.

We have built the model in stages, firstly focusing on the most significant area: budget share, which for academies is the core element of General Annual Grant. Once we have established the three final scenarios for this element, we will add in other sources of funding.

Having constructed the model, you will be able to roll it forward to achieve a continuous three-year forecast, simply by changing the baseline to reflect the new year's actual funding and reviewing the percentage changes for subsequent years.

There are several steps to take to convert the two elements of per-pupil funding and rolls to a set of best, middle and worst-case scenarios for your budget share or GAG. We will guide you through these steps in detail, but for now they can be summarised as follows:

1. Establish your latest funding per-pupil. Due to the timing of this book's publication, we anticipate that for most of you this will be your 2019/20 allocation.

    If you are coming to this later and wish to make your first year 2020/21 but have not yet received your allocation, follow our method with 2019/20 as your first year, but roll the model on for three years beyond that instead of two, then update it when your new funding statement arrives.

2. Identify the element of funding relating to pupil characteristics (i.e. affected by rolls). School-led items such as lump sums and premises costs need to be excluded, but they will be added back later.

3. For each option, estimate the percentage change in this per-pupil funding in the following two years. We provide guidance on how to do this at the appropriate point.

4. Set your baseline rolls using census data from the October before the start of the first financial year in the model, i.e. October 2018 for 2019/20. This is the data on which your funding is calculated, not the current academic year rolls.

5. For each option, estimate the pupil numbers you are likely to have in the following two years, again using the funded roll from the previous October. You can roll forward the baseline set of year groups and estimate each new intake year, applying a turnover allowance if you have high pupil mobility.

Alternatively, you can input estimated rolls directly into the model.

6. Match up each of the per-pupil funding and rolls options with each other. This will create nine different combinations as we showed in the diagram in the previous chapter. Then you will need to add back the items you excluded from step 1.

7. From these nine, choose your final three scenarios. Your choice will depend on how confident you are about either per-pupil funding or rolls, and whether there is enough of a distance between the three alternatives to make the different budget plans meaningful.

Once you have reached this stage, you can add in best, middle and worst-case estimates for your other funding sources to complete the final three scenarios. You can use your local knowledge to produce estimates for Pupil Premium, funding for nursery or post-16, and additional allocations for pupils with SEND, as appropriate to your situation.

We have included some guidance on these additional funding sources, but your local circumstances may be quite different, so we can't be prescriptive about the approach to take.

Any other government grants that you receive should be built into the model too. However, it's important not to include any self-generated income such as donations and charges for lettings and traded services. These items of income will be deducted from your gross spending to calculate net expenditure, which you will measure against the funding forecasts in your budget plans. If you include self-generated income as funding, you risk double counting it.

Information requirements

The main information that you will need in order to make a start on setting up the model will be your most up-to-date funding statement (2019/20 in our example). This will show details of the relevant October census data on which that funding is based (October 2018 for 2019/20). If you want to be prepared for all stages of the model, find your 2017/18 budget statement; we will be using this to decide on the percentage changes for per-pupil funding later.

These statements provide the information you need to set up the forecasting model. You will also need the breakdown of the October 2018 pupil number data for your school by year group as well as Ever 6 Free School Meal eligibility, to enable you to create projections of funded pupil numbers for the three-year period and an estimate of Pupil Premium Grant.

We have designed the model in a way that minimises the amount of input you need to do, once you have set up the formulae. Most of the calculations feed off baseline information that you enter once, using your estimated percentage changes to build the scenarios. It's a flexible approach, which allows you to change your assumptions quite quickly and see the results updating automatically.

Each chapter of this book will guide you through a different element of the process. In the case of the per-pupil funding and roll projections, we provide separate chapters to guide you in arriving at your assumptions for the annual percentage changes in values.

Some of the information is fairly technical in nature, but we guide you through the most important points. For example, we will show you where to find illustrative allocations for the National Funding Formula when it is fully implemented, and we will guide you in how to interpret the information. We will also explain the choices your LA has about whether or how far to implement the NFF locally.

In other cases, we will provide prompts for you to consider, such as what the main influences might be on your future rolls, or who you could contact to find out about population changes and plans for housing developments.

Tailoring the model

Throughout this book we offer our thoughts on an appropriate style for the model, but naturally you are free to tailor it to your own preferences and circumstances. Take time to consider what would best suit your ways of working.

As we embark on the activities, we will provide a link from which you can download a PDF with screen shots of our own model as an example, to make it easier to follow the methodology. This is for your personal use as guidance for preparing your own model, and we would ask you to respect our work by not sharing it with others who haven't bought the book; anyone using it without the guidance may make erroneous assumptions. You are not permitted to distribute it or exploit it for commercial purposes.

There are many different ways of tailoring the model, either in substance or in presentation. Your school may have a house style for working documents, or you might have a personal style and preference for how you build spreadsheets.

As an example, you could vary the number of years covered in the model or choose two or four options instead of three. You can also tweak the different elements. For example, we provide guidance on issues to consider for funding streams such as Pupil Premium, but if they are not a significant source of funding in your school, you may not want to spend much time on it.

The model needs to work for you, so don't be afraid to experiment with the best presentation and content. You may be able to find a better way. But please check carefully to make sure that all the calculations work and that any cross-referencing between sheets within the workbook is accurate. We can't take responsibility for any errors in building the model.

Here are our top tips to help you construct your model:

- Keep notes as you go, recording any changes you make to the method. For example, if you decide not to use the turnover allowance in the rolls projection, preferring instead to enter year group sizes directly, keep a note of how you have estimated them. At the appropriate time, you can then easily transfer the details into your Financial Sustainability Plan to explain your assumptions.
- Imagine someone else needs to take it over in the future - will they be able to follow what you've done? It may take you a while to reach the stage of producing your Financial Sustainability Plan, so it's sensible to make notes as you go. You can always leave your copy of this book, but a local set of instructions is best, especially if you have tailored the model.

- Carry out a sense check of the final results. Do they look reasonable? Can you easily pinpoint the main reasons for the differences between scenarios, or do some aspects look odd? Watch out for errors in entering data or percentage changes.
- Always double check any links between cells on a sheet or between sheets in the workbook.
- Use absolute values to fix a cell in a formula where you want to copy it into other cells without losing the reference to a particular cell's value. In case you don't know this trick, pressing the F4 key once fixes both the column and row numbers, a second time fixes the row number only and a third press fixes the column number only.
- Colour code your cells where you need to enter data, so they stand out. We used different colours for input cells, referenced or calculated cells, and those which are totals.
- If you really want to avoid messing up the file accidentally, lock cells that hold calculations and when you have finished building the model, protect the sheets with a password so that you are unable to overwrite them. You will then only be able to enter data into unlocked cells. We explain how to do this later.
- <u>Please</u> make sure you save your work regularly, preferably backing it up to the cloud and saving it on an external drive just to be sure.

Remember that the model isn't a fixed tool that you do once and then forget about. Being flexible is essential for financial sustainability. Whenever new information becomes available, particularly during the LA's budget setting process, you should revisit the model and consider whether the percentage changes for each year need to be amended, or whether you have selected the most appropriate three final scenarios from the nine options.

4 PER-PUPIL FUNDING PROJECTIONS

Making a start

In this chapter, we will show you how to build the first stage of the model. It involves setting up a baseline calculation for the amount per pupil you are receiving in your most up-to-date allocation. You will then be able to move this on for the following two years by applying an annual percentage change.

Once you have created this template, you will replicate it to achieve three versions: your best, middle and worst-case options for per-pupil funding.

At this stage, we are not going to go into how you can arrive at your decisions on the percentage change in funding for each year. This chapter is about the mechanics of setting up the tool.

We have made our system efficient by showing you how to reference key items so that you only need to enter data once. When it's set up correctly, certain fields will be calculated automatically. This will save you a lot of time when you want to adjust your options to test out the impact of different assumptions.

If you are an experienced Excel user, you will probably know how you want to build the model once you've read our introductory sections at each stage, where we explain what is being created. You are free to go ahead in your own way and skip our detailed descriptions, which are written for those who want a step-by-step guide. We have deliberately used simple formulae to make it easier for anyone who isn't an advanced user. If you are familiar with other lookup functions such as INDEX and MATCH, for example, feel free to use them.

The first thing you need to do is find your budget share or GAG funding statement for the latest year. All of our examples are based on the baseline year being 2019/20, with forecasts for 2020/21 and 2021/22. However, it's a flexible model; you can set it up to reflect whatever three-year period you are working on.

If you are embarking on this nearer to the end of 2019, you are probably looking to develop a forecast for the period 2020/21 to 2022/23 before you have received your 2020/21 allocations. In that case, you can still use 2019/20 as the baseline year and simply extend the period by one year. Once you receive your actual 2020/21 allocation, you will be able to update the model.

Your first worksheet in the new Excel file you create will be the best-case scenario for the level of per pupil funding you will receive. This will hold the basic information and method for the per pupil funding element of the options. Once you're happy with it, you can replicate it for the middle and worst-case options. You will then only need to alter the percentage change for each year in those worksheets.

This is your model, and you need to make it work for you. As we have done with our exemplar model, you can adopt some formatting principles to make it clear for anyone else using it in the future.

Blank tables are provided in the book to guide you in constructing the model, and the activities contain descriptions of the relevant formulae and how to reference other parts of the model. If you want to see detailed examples, we have created a PDF of screen shots from our own model, which you can download by going to this link:

https://bit.ly/2SzA7q2

Activity

Activity 1: Setting up your Best £ per pupil worksheet

- In Sheet 1, create a heading 'Best £ per pupil' and edit the worksheet tab to show the same name.
- Set up row descriptors for the different elements of your funding, as shown in the example on the next page.
- Set up columns for the baseline year and the following two years, as shown in the example. Tailor the year headings if

necessary to match the period you are working on. We have shaded the cells for years 2 and 3 in rows 4-12 where you don't need to enter figures.

- If you wish, colour code the worksheet to distinguish input cells from those with formulae or totals. This can help you to avoid overwriting formulae accidentally. For a more robust method, see our notes on locking cells at the end of this chapter.
- You can create grid lines and other formatting styles to make the table look more professional. This is up to you; the spreadsheet shows your background workings, but you may want to take a screenshot of it to include in your Financial Sustainability Plan.

	A	B	C	D	E
1		Best Case Scenario - £ per pupil before MFG excluded items			
2	Item		2019/20	2020/21	2021/22
3			£	£	£
4	1	School's budget share/GAG in baseline year (after MFG and capping but before LA school de-delegation or MAT top slice is deducted)			
5					
6	2	Baseline year rates			
7	3	Baseline year lump sum and sparsity factors			
8	4	Baseline year additional lump sum for amalgamating schools			
9	5	Agreed MFG exclusions and technical adjustments			
10	6	Total of excluded items			
11	7	MFG baseline (1 - 6)			
12	8	Funded number on roll from baseline year statement (excluding reception uplift where used)			
13	9	MFG Baseline value per pupil (7 / 8)			
14	10	Estimated % change in per pupil funding			
15	11	% Multiplier for funding			
16	12	Estimated value per pupil (item 9 x item 11)			

******

Creating per-pupil funding for the baseline year

The first thing you need to do is enter the baseline figures on which your three-year projections will be based. As already noted, the examples we have developed start with a baseline year of 2019/20 and build forecasts for 2020/21 and 2021/22.

The method we have used is based on the Minimum Funding Guarantee (MFG) calculation, which defines the lowest possible level of funding that you can legally receive. The MFG percentage is therefore a valid starting point for the worst-case option.

This calculation isolates the pupil-led items within the funding formula for your baseline year. The government requires at least 80% of funding to be pupil-led, so this element is the one that most affects your allocation. You start with budget share or GAG and deduct school-led items such as rates (LA schools only as GAG doesn't include rates), the lump sum, any one-off additional lump sum from an amalgamation, and sparsity funding.

A very small number of schools may have some technical adjustments for unusual items. You are likely to know if this applies to you, as they are exceptional and tend to relate to specific features in your school. After deducting these, the remaining pupil-led cash total is converted to an amount per pupil, representing your baseline per-pupil funding.

This figure is the foundation for your forecasts. You will choose three different sets of percentage changes to create best, middle and worst-case options for years two and three.

The school-led items will be added back at a later stage, so don't worry about those for the moment.

Our instructions refer to the cell numbering in our PDF example document.

Activity 2: Entering baseline figures

- Item 1: in the column for 2019/20 at cell C4, enter your total budget share, or for academies, the item 1 total school allocation from your GAG statement. This should be the pre-16 formula total, before any de-delegation (LA schools) or MAT top slice (academies).
  Don't include any other items of funding or grants that sit outside the formula, e.g. nursery, post-16 or top-ups for SEN.

Your budget share/GAG includes the notional SEN budget that pays for the first £6,000 of specialist support for each pupil with SEN. It does not include extra top-up allocations for Education Health and Care Plans (EHCPs) or non-plan SEN funding for individual children above the £6,000 threshold; we will add these at a much later stage in the model.

- Items 2 to 5: in the 2019/20 column, enter in cells C6 to C9 the amounts listed as they appear on your funding statement. You will be deducting these from the top line very soon.

  These items are the school-led elements of the formula which are currently specified by the DfE as being outside of the Minimum Funding Guarantee (MFG). As you roll forward the baseline in later years, you will need to check for any changes in the MFG calculation and amend the excluded items.

  NB if you are an academy, don't enter rates into the exclusions list. The GAG amount in the top row already excludes rates.
- Item 6: in cell C10, create a subtotal for the excluded items by adding together the figures in cells C6:C9.
- Item 7: in cell C11, create a formula to deduct item 6 (cell C10) from the funding at item 1 (cell C4), leaving the budget share/GAG less MFG exclusions as the baseline.
- Item 8: enter into cell C12 the total funded rolls for your relevant year groups between Reception and Y11 as shown in your baseline year's funding statement, e.g. October 2018 for 2019/20. These are <u>funded</u> pupils, not the actual pupils to be taught in the year in question.
- Item 9: in cell C13, insert a formula to divide item 7 (cell C11) by the item 8 roll (cell C12). This expresses the pupil-led funding as a per pupil amount for the baseline year.

Our PDF example will help you check your workings for this first stage. In that document, we have combined the examples for activities 2 and 3, since activity 3 (which follows) is merely the completion of the last four rows of the table.

******

Your per-pupil funding options

The next stage is to set up the progression of your per-pupil funding across the second and third years for the best-case option. Once this is ready, you are going to replicate it for the middle and worst-case options.

Activity 3: Setting up calculated fields for all years

In this activity, you will enter the calculations to create an updated pupil-led value per pupil for the next two years. This will prepare the model ready for you to enter the percentage changes, once you have worked through our guidance in the next two chapters.

We will start with the last four rows of column D for 2020/21, again using the cell references from our PDF example.

- In cell D13, enter =C13 to pick up the baseline per-pupil figure.
- Format the data entry cell in cell D14 as a percentage, ready for you to enter the percentage change in 2020/21 later on. This will be applied to the baseline year in order to estimate how much each pupil will attract in the second year.
- In cell D15, create a formula for the multiplier: =100%+D14 (formatted as a percentage). If you enter 2% in line 14, this will produce a value of 102%, and if you enter a negative of -1.5%, it will show 98.5%.
- Create a formula in cell D16, formatted as currency to two decimal points, to multiply the baseline value in cell D13 by the multiplier in D15 that you created in the last step. This should give you the estimated pupil-led value for 2020/21 in the final cell.

Now repeat the process for 2021/22, but with one important difference. In cell E13, you need to pick up the 2020/21 estimated value per pupil from the bottom of the previous column as the starting point, i.e. referencing cell D16.

Once you are confident the formulae are working in this sheet and you are happy with the formatting, it's time to copy the sheet to create your middle and worst-case options.

- Right click on the Best £ per pupil worksheet tab at the bottom of the sheet and select Move or Copy, clicking on the box 'Create a Copy'.
- Select the positioning which places it after the Best £ per pupil worksheet and click OK.
- Change this second worksheet tab to Middle £ per pupil.
- Repeat the above process, placing the new sheet at the end.
- Rename the third worksheet tab Worst £ per pupil.
- Amend the headings at the top of the middle and worst sheets.

Extra tip:

Once you have finished setting up a worksheet, have tested it and are happy with the format, it is advisable to lock cells that contain formulae to avoid overwriting them and causing errors.

Note that for these first three £ per pupil sheets, you should not lock data entry cells, especially not those in row 14 where you enter the percentage changes, as you need to be able to amend these at any time.

Here are the instructions if you need them:

- Select the cells you want to lock, holding down the Ctrl key for multiple selections, and with a right mouse click, select Format Cells. In the Protection tab, click the box for Lock Cells and click OK. Alternatively, you can use the Cells toolbar on the Home tab and click on the downward arrow for Format then select Lock Cell.
- The locking of cells will not take effect until you protect the whole sheet through either the Home/Cells/Format/Protect Sheet menu, or the Review/Protect Sheet menu. If you wish, you can select various options to allow the user to perform certain functions. Then choose a password and confirm it. Don't forget the password, or you won't be able to amend any of the locked cells if you later want to change the formulae or formatting.

- Test out whether you have locked the correct cells by trying to enter data in them; you should see a message telling you they are locked.

******

Now you're ready to consider what percentage changes you want to enter. Our next chapter will provide some clues to help you.

5 THE CONTEXT FOR PER-PUPIL FUNDING

Areas to consider

Your assumptions on how your per-pupil funding will change in future are vitally important to the model's results. They need to be as robust as possible, with a clear rationale for your choices.

This is the trickiest part of building the model, because the funding reforms have introduced complications and uncertainties. Consequently, we will be spending quite a lot of time on this. Don't worry - the rest of the model will be less intensive. Putting in the groundwork on your per-pupil funding is definitely worth the effort; it underpins everything else.

We have broken this area up into two chapters. This chapter will provide an outline of the main issues and the next one will provide specific guidance on how to choose your percentage changes for the per-pupil funding part of the model, as appropriate to your situation.

Ignore any thoughts about how changes in your total rolls might affect your funding for now – in this first stage, we are focusing solely on how much funding you are likely to receive per pupil.

As with our other funding guides in the series, we encourage you to be selective in which elements of our advice you use, according to your own needs and knowledge.

The weightings you give to different pieces of information will be a matter of judgement, taking your local circumstances into account. There are no right and wrong answers, as long as you have a sensible rationale for your choices and they provide a reasonable fit for best, middle and worst-case options.

As you develop your understanding of the model, you will be able to step back and get a different perspective on the results; new ideas might emerge. Remember that you can go back and change the figures at a later stage if you want to.

Here is a brief run down of the main items we would encourage you to think about, before we start to examine them in more detail.

- Your **starting point** in terms of the funding you currently receive, compared to the NFF values.
- **National influences:** decisions taken by central government on the amount of funding available and how it is distributed to local authorities. Government will determine all allocations directly when the 'Hard NFF' is introduced.
- **Local influences:** decisions by local authorities during the period of the 'Soft NFF' when local formulae are still used to share out the funding between schools. This includes decisions to apply any DSG reserves from previous years, although these will only provide a one-off boost. Where the LA is experiencing pressures in the High Needs Budget, it may be necessary to make a transfer of funding from the Schools Block, which will reduce the amount available for the formula.
- **Schools Forum decisions** on retention of funding centrally, where some services may cease, freeing up money for the formula.
- **Pupil characteristics**, such as deprivation, prior attainment, EAL and pupil mobility. Total pupil numbers will be important when you build your roll projections in the next stage of the process. But your pupil characteristics could influence the amount per pupil you receive, especially if you are more dependent on certain factors whose values are changing significantly.

Your starting point

An important consideration in forecasting the progression of your average funding per pupil over the next three years is what your current situation looks like compared to the ultimate destination, i.e. the government's NFF values.

It's vital to bear in mind that the government's decisions under the 'Soft NFF' relate to the grant that the DfE gives to LAs. The local authority in your area may take different decisions, as we will see in later sections.

The NFF has introduced turbulence into the school funding system through the adoption of a consistent formula across England. This replaces a system that was built on historical levels of DSG and local decisions on its distribution between schools.

Most commentators agree that the old system needed to change; the issues are the amount of funding in the system and the way in which it's been distributed.

The ideal approach would have been to level up the worst funded schools. The government has chosen not to do this, so if the pure formula were introduced without any protections, schools which historically have had higher funding levels would see reductions.

Because this would cause massive job losses and pose a risk to children's education, the new system had to involve a transitional approach that smoothed the change over several years.

The form this takes is protection for schools that would otherwise see significant losses in funding. Under the original proposals, schools could have faced a reduction from the previous year of up to 1.5% per pupil per year, with a maximum loss (floor) of -3%. However, in July 2017 the DfE announced an improved level of protection, increasing DSG by £1.3bn from other departmental budgets.

The extra money meant that in 2018/19 and 2019/20, the grant to LAs was based on a **minimum increase of at least 0.5% per year for every school** in their area. A Minimum Funding Level was also introduced (MFL - not to be confused with the Minimum Funding Guarantee), providing a minimum cash figure, varying by sector, for schools who are reliant on the basic funding entitlements in the formula, i.e. those with low additional needs.

The cost of protection is partly funded by limiting (capping) gains for those schools who benefit from the NFF. In the first two years, **gains have been capped at 3% per pupil per year**. Over time the cap will lift, so that underfunded schools eventually reach the pure formula. The time taken to do so will vary, depending on how far away from the NFF a school's 2017/18 baseline funding was, and the pace at which the government or LAs decide to lift the cap. That in turn depends on the overall level of funding available. It's a delicate balancing act.

These transitional arrangements slow the pace of change. We will talk more about this in the section on national and local influences, but for now we suggest you look at your latest funding statement and compare the unit values for each factor to the NFF values, to understand how far away from the NFF your starting point is.

Here are the 2019/20 national unit values:

Factor	Primary value	Secondary value
Basic per pupil (AWPU) Primary	£2,747	
AWPU KS3		£3,863
AWPU KS4		£4,386
Current FSM	£440	£440
Ever6 FSM	£540	£785
IDACI Band F	£200	£290
IDACI Band E	£240	£390
IDACI Band D	£360	£515
IDACI Band C	£390	£560
IDACI Band B	£420	£600
IDACI Band A	£575	£810
Low prior attainment	£1,022	£1,550
English as an Additional Language	£515	£1,385
Lump sum	£110,000	£110,000
Sparsity (max)	£25,000	£65,000

The values were set for the first two years, so all have remained the same as in 2018/19, with one exception. The primary low prior attainment factor has been reduced very slightly from £1,050 to £1,022. The DfE explains this in the policy document:

'The LPA cohort in primary schools that we measure for school funding purposes has been increasing over the past six years, because of changes made to the Early Years Foundation Stage Profile in 2013. This increase comes from changes to the assessment, rather than changes to the underlying level of need. Therefore, we are *maintaining the total proportion of spend on primary LPA through the formula by balancing the increase in the eligible cohort with a reduction in the factor value.'*

Knowing the gap between the amount the pure NFF would provide and your current funding will enable you to picture the general trajectory your funding is likely to take in the longer term. This will help you in developing your strategy for a sustainable budget. We will cover the potential options for transition in a later section.

It's important to understand the intentions of the government and your local authority when estimating the likely pattern of your future funding. It isn't an exact science, but you would be wise to take a disciplined approach. By this we mean you should resist the temptation to create a forecast of what you'd like your funding to be, rather than what it could be.

Let's now explore further the different national and local approaches to school funding to help you think about the various options for the future.

National influences

There are two aspects to government decisions on school funding: the amount of money placed into the national pot, and the DfE's distribution of it between local authorities.

The level of available funding

The government is fond of stating that school funding has never been higher, but the reason is that the number of pupils in education has never been higher. Ministers also claim to be protecting funding in real terms across 2018/19 and 2019/20. This takes us up to the end of the current Spending Review period. During 2019, the Treasury will draw up plans for the next set of allocations to government departments from April 2020.

However, the truth is that the 2017/18 baseline which is being protected is completely inadequate, due to the significant level of unfunded cost pressures during the previous three years. The Secretary of State, Damian Hinds, has confirmed that there were real terms cuts between 2015/16 and 2017/18, and reports by the National Audit Office and Education Policy Institute provide evidence of this.

There have been various attempts to draw attention to the shortfall in funding for schools, but the reality is that we will have to wait for the Spending Review 2019 to find out what the prognosis is from 2020 onwards.

As you develop your multi-year budget plans, you should bear in mind that there could be an impact on mainstream school budgets as a result of the difficulties that LAs are experiencing following the introduction of the High Needs National Funding Formula. You can refer to your area's SEND Local Offer website to discover the actions your LA is proposing as a result of their High Needs review.

Julie posted an article on our School Financial Success blog in November 2018 which outlined the main issues in relation to high needs. If you are interested in this, take a look at the following link: https://schoolfinancialsuccess.com/high-needs-funding-in-crisis/.

It will probably be some time before we know whether all the lobbying has been successful in securing more money for education, and if it is, how the DfE plans to allocate it.

We therefore advise you not to make any overly optimistic assumptions about the potential for any future improvements in funding. It's the end of a very challenging period for government finances and the overriding focus is on Brexit.

As further information becomes available, you will be able to tweak your forecasts accordingly, but a prudent approach will serve you best in these early stages.

Distribution of funding from the DfE to LAs: NFF factors

The second area of national influence is the distribution of the available funding from the DfE to local authorities. Under the 'Soft NFF', the DfE calculates the NFF formula (including the transitional protection and capping already mentioned) for individual schools and aggregates them up to local authority level. Other non-formula items are added, which we will refer to later.

Our focus here is on the amount of funding allocated per pupil. We will consider the impact of changes in pupil numbers later.

There are some challenges in looking beyond 2019/20, because we don't know whether the NFF factor values will be changed in 2020/21. There is also an annual update of the data that is used to convert the NFF into per-pupil units of funding.

While growth in pupil numbers doesn't in itself alter the units of funding, because the higher allocation is divided by more pupils, it's possible that the blend of pupil characteristics could cause some slight changes.

You can see why we say it's not particularly easy to forecast per-pupil funding levels. But we have to make some educated guesses, otherwise there is no basis for our three-year plans. You'll be forgiven if forecasts based on robust assumptions aren't quite accurate, but you could run into trouble if you don't even attempt a forecast.

In the absence of any further information, we would suggest that the NFF factor values are likely to remain the same in 2020/21, unless the government finds substantially more funding for schools.

The unit values could increase if pay grants to support the teachers' pay award from September 2018 and increases in employer contribution to the Teachers Pension Scheme from 2019 are absorbed into the formula. But that won't change the overall level of funding, as it's just being moved from one pot to another. We'd expect the extra funding to be added to the baseline for transition. However, transferring these grants into the Schools Block could result in a redistribution of the money.

For schools that are due to gain from the NFF, we believe it's a reasonable assumption that the DfE will want to continue to lift the cap at a similar rate to the current 3% per year. From our assessment of the information published by the DfE, it appears that if the current approach does continue, most of the schools with gains are likely to reach the pure formula by 2021/22. It therefore seems unlikely that the government would change the approach.

This is an example of the sort of thinking you can do to arrive at your own assumptions.

A rather more difficult question is whether protection will continue at the minimum increase of 0.5% per year in the new Spending Review period. This will largely depend on whether the extra £1.3bn is going to be built into the baseline for 2020/21 onwards.

Please remember that throughout this section, we are referring to the amount of grant paid to local authorities. LAs might not replicate this transition when passing the money on; we will explore this when we discuss local influences.

There is another element within the DSG allocations to LAs which sits outside the core NFF. It concerns items referred to as historic spend factors.

Distribution of funding from the DfE to LAs: historic spend factors

We mentioned earlier that the distribution of grant doesn't only involve the NFF factors. There are some items that don't lend themselves to a formulaic approach: premises costs such as non-domestic rates, split site and Private Finance Initiative (PFI) costs, pupil mobility and growth in pupil numbers. When the Department is directly funding over 24,000 schools and academies, it won't want to be involved in negotiating allocations at an individual school level.

As an interim measure prior to the Hard NFF being introduced, these items are being funded on the basis of the previous year's planned spending by each LA, hence the term historic spend factors. The only exception is PFI, where an inflationary uplift is applied (3.83% in 2018/19 and 3.36% in 2019/20).

Within the historic spend category, academies don't currently need to worry about rates, as they are dealt with by ESFA.

There is no guarantee that the actual costs for these items will be the same as in the previous year. This is one of the reasons LAs might have cost pressures to manage within the formula, but it's also possible that some may have savings.

Although the government has reviewed some of the historic spend items to explore the potential for bringing them into the NFF in 2019/20, only one new factor has been identified: pupil number growth.

For 2019/20, the new growth factor has been calculated by comparing the October 2018 census data with the equivalent data for 2017. LAs received final details of their allocation in the December 2018 DSG settlement.

The DfE has applied a national average unit cost per extra pupil to the data, but LAs are free to determine their own values and eligibility criteria (within a broad framework set by the DfE) in any local growth fund they choose to operate.

Some LAs may have had growth funds for primary schools in previous years and are now likely to extend these funds to cover secondary school growth. The intention is to fund significant increases to meet basic need, such as a whole extra year group. Marginal changes each September still have to be funded by schools and academies until the start of the next financial year.

Let's now look at the local influences on your future funding. This may prompt you to ask some questions of your local authority or Schools Forum representatives as you are developing your assumptions.

Local influences

Under the Soft NFF, LAs can choose to move partially or fully towards the national factor values, or they can ignore them. This is a fundamental issue which will directly affect your school's funding until at least March 2021 for LA schools and August 2021 for academies. It means that you need to be aware of the local strategy in order to build it into your per-pupil funding projections.

We can now see how LAs responded to this freedom in the first year of the NFF: the DfE has published an analysis of LA decisions on their local formulae in 2018/19 in July 2018. It can be found at:

https://www.gov.uk/government/publications/schools-block-funding-formulae-2018-to-2019.

Here you will find a PDF document which provides an analysis of the results, together with an Excel workbook containing the detailed formula values and data for every LA.

The analysis document highlights that 73 out of 150 LAs have moved every one of their factor values closer to the NFF and 41 of them have implemented the NFF fully. What matters is whether your LA was one of them or not.

Local decisions on progress towards the NFF

Since the NFF was introduced, the majority of LAs have moved towards it when setting their local factor values. A few LAs have decided to keep their existing formula, but the amount of grant available to fund it will almost certainly have changed, due to the NFF now being used to calculate each LA's funding.

Some LAs may have wished to move towards the NFF in 2018/19 and 2019/20 but were not able to do so. There are various reasons why this might be the case, but the main three are:

- Historic spend items may have increased in cost. These pressures will eat into the funding available for the formula factors and transitional protection.
- There could be deficits in centrally retained budgets which have to be the first call on the Schools Budget, subject to agreement from the Schools Forum.
- There may be pressures in the High Needs Budget which require a transfer from the Schools Block of no more than 0.5%, reducing the amount available for the formula. The Schools Forum has to approve the transfer. If more than 0.5% is needed, the Secretary of State has to approve it, even if the Schools Forum agrees.

In relation to the last two of these points, the DfE is planning more stringent monitoring for LAs with deficits in the overall DSG. LAs will have to report on any deficits above 1% at March 2019 and provide details of their recovery plans.

Transition

While we are in the Soft NFF phase, it is up to the LA to decide how far to smooth the impact of changes in the local formula on individual schools from one year to the next.

Knowing how your LA has decided to do this is vitally important, because this will affect the pace at which you and the other schools in your area will move towards the NFF values (if they haven't already been adopted). This is true for academies as well as LA maintained schools, since the local formula is the basis for every school's funding under the Soft NFF.

If an LA is struggling to balance the local formula within the available grant, there are two main options to resolve it which involve adjusting transitional arrangements:

- They could revert to the statutory Minimum Funding Guarantee protection level (a loss of up to 1.5% per pupil per year) instead of using the new freedom to improve it. LAs can set the MFG anywhere between -1.5% and the NFF +0.5% per pupil per year without asking for permission from the Secretary of State.
- They could implement a lower cap than the NFF figure, i.e. restrict gains to somewhere between 0% and 3%.

The published file containing all LA funding formulae for 2018/19 shows that 62 out of 150 LAs replicated the NFF minimum increase of 0.5%. The others used a range of protection and capping levels to balance the formula to the available funding.

Release of DSG reserves

Local authorities are able to carry forward surplus DSG, which can only come from savings in central budgets (since schools are allowed to carry forward their balances). If this is not needed for High Needs or other pressures, it can be paid into the formula pot.

If reserves are transferred into the funding formula, it will be a one-off exercise. Make sure you don't count them again in future years when forecasting your funding, as they can only be used once.

There can be quite a time lag before reserves become available, because of the timing between budget setting and closure of accounts. Budget decisions need to be taken by Christmas, because the LA has to submit its formula to the DfE in the third week of January. At this point, the previous year end's results will be known, but the current year's can only be estimated. LAs will be cautious about committing these for redistribution, in case unexpected expenditure occurs in the spring term.

LAs are not permitted to adjust school budget shares during the year, because there isn't an equivalent process for ESFA to do the same for academies. The only exceptions are adjustments for Early Years, High Needs and rates funding, and specific funds held centrally (e.g. growth, falling rolls and schools in financial difficulty).

Some LAs may have savings in historic spend items, which can be redirected to other factors in the formula. These won't increase the overall pot, as the money is already in the formula, but it may enable the LA to improve other factor values. They may even go above the NFF values.

If any of the above situations occur, the distribution of additional funding may mean that some schools no longer trigger protection. However, it won't make any difference to those who are subject to capping, as they aren't allowed to receive any further increases above the level of the cap.

Your LA might have been in a favourable position in the latest settlement, but it doesn't automatically mean that surplus funding will be available in future years. There could be turbulence in historic spend factors, where either local costs vary from the previous year, or where the DfE manages to turn them into formulaic factors in future years.

The operation of the formula can be a delicate balancing act for an LA. For every decision to move money between factors or to alter the level of protection or capping, allocations will change, and a different number of schools will come in or out of the transitional arrangements. It's usually an iterative process which ends when the overall formula is balanced to the available resources in the fairest way possible.

LAs are expected to discuss their intentions with the Schools Forum before political approval is sought. If you are asked for your opinion in budget consultation exercises for future years, we would encourage you to take up the opportunity to have your say.

Schools Forum decisions on central budgets

Schools Forums can take decisions which might increase the amount of money available in the formula. These are relatively minor in terms of the amounts involved, because the government's focus has been on maximising delegated funding to schools. There isn't much flexibility left in other funds.

The main area where this might happen is where budget reductions are agreed by the Forum for services funded from the Central School Services Block (CSSB). Many of these items originated from historic Forum decisions to support school improvement through a centralised set of services or to enter into contracts with the intention of providing economies of scale and better value for money.

The DfE intends to reduce the historic commitments element of this block from 2020/21 if it doesn't see expenditure 'unwinding'. However, it is believed that when this change happens, the funding will go back into the national pot rather than being redistributed locally, as it is now.

Decisions on central budgets are usually taken around November or December each year. Anyone can attend Schools Forum meetings as an observer, so we recommend that you go and listen to the debate in the next budget cycle. If you can't spare the time to attend the meetings, make sure your representatives on the Forum provide regular updates to network meetings. Papers and minutes recording the decisions should be available on a public-facing website.

Pupil characteristics

We have already touched upon the time lag in the data used to calculate the amount per primary and secondary pupil within your LA's DSG. But there is a more localised issue in relation to the make-up of your school population.

While we are in the Soft NFF stage with a local formula, your funding is influenced by how your data behaves in relation to the data of other schools and academies in your local area. This relativity is important, although we should bear in mind that the majority of funding is allocated on pure pupil numbers.

When local formulae were in a steady state, with factor values generally maintained from one year to the next, it was fairly easy to tell how your budget might change in response to particular characteristics. As an example, if the total pupils eligible for free school meals broadly stayed the same, but yours reduced, you were likely to see a reduction in your FSM funding. If data increased overall, the LA had a choice of freezing the pot - which reduced the unit value - or increasing the pot and maintaining the unit value.

In the current climate of turbulence in factor values due to the NFF (with each LA taking its own decisions) and rapid growth in rolls in many areas, it is very difficult to predict what will happen to your funding. Even if your data is static for a particular factor, you might get a smaller allocation, either because other schools have higher eligibility and the pot has to be frozen for affordability reasons, or because the factor value has changed. This could be a matter of policy, e.g. to mirror the NFF or prioritise a particular issue.

It's important to be aware of any areas where your school is highly reliant on particular factors. It's especially vital to know what the difference is between your local values and the NFF values for those factors. This provides an indication of what might happen to your funding once the DfE funds all schools directly using the NFF.

In most LAs, it is very difficult to make generalisations about which types of schools have gained or lost from the NFF, because the relationship between data and unit values has become more complex.

The local sector ratio

Another issue which is worth mentioning is the local difference in funding between the sectors, i.e. the ratio between primary and secondary per-pupil funding. This currently varies significantly between LAs, from 1:1.16 to 1:1.58, i.e. secondary funding is between 16% and 58% higher per pupil than primary funding. Your local ratio could change as a result of the NFF, which might mean schools in one sector could gain and those in another may have to rely on protection. You have probably already experienced this if your authority has moved towards the national factor values.

These ratios have developed over time and for various reasons. In the past, some LAs benefited from the Excellence in Cities programme, which awarded significant sums to secondary schools in areas of high deprivation. Eventually, these grants were merged into the local formulae, which increased the ratio in favour of secondary schools.

At various points in the past, there will have been particular priorities in some LAs, such as addressing standards in one sector or the other, which may have influenced the relativity of funding between the sectors.

Do you know what the local ratio is for your LA's formula? The Excel file mentioned previously, which accompanies the DfE analysis of 2018/19 funding formulae, contains this information in columns HH and HI.

If your ratio is significantly different to the average of 1:1.29, it could be an indication of how your sector will fare as we move towards the Hard NFF.

The NFF calculations behind the allocations of grant to LAs produce an individual primary:secondary ratio for each authority. They depend on the balance of pupil numbers, characteristics between the sectors, the values that are attached to those factors and which type of schools qualify for protection. It could take some time for your LA's ratio to shift, because of the protection arrangements.

We hope this rundown of the issues to consider helps you to appreciate the national and local contexts for your future funding. Now we will look more specifically at your task of identifying the percentage changes to enter into your model.

6 DECIDING ON PER-PUPIL FUNDING CHANGES

The challenge ahead

We recognise that it's not easy to draw conclusions from the above information, so in this chapter we're going to try to boil it down to the main possibilities and see what they mean for your choice of per-pupil funding options across the three years. We can provide guidelines to help you consider the most appropriate percentage changes to apply to your per-pupil funding in years two and three of the model, but the decision is yours.

Of necessity, this chapter is quite complex. There are all sorts of reasons behind the funding changes for individual schools, and you will need to work out which of them apply to your situation. Take it slowly, and make sure you understand each point before going on to the next. We can't know what circumstances you are in, so this chapter has to explain the possibilities in a methodical way.

Once you've worked through this chapter, you'll have made great strides in understanding not only the potential changes to your future funding, but also the reasons behind them. The rest of the model is pretty straightforward compared to this, so you should feel a real sense of accomplishment when you have arrived at the percentage changes for your per-pupil funding.

What information is relevant?

Fortunately, there is a source of information for the long-term NFF results which you can use to start off the process of deciding on your estimated percentage changes. We will be comparing your eventual destination with the percentage change you have received in your actual

2019/20 allocation compared to your 2017/18 baseline, i.e. before the NFF began.

Once you can see how far away your current funding is from the pure formula, you will be able to spread the residual changes over the next two years, according to your assumptions on the rate of transition.

The DfE has provided a file showing the results of the NFF calculation for every school as a basis for 2019/20 DSG allocations to LAs. These calculations are aggregated to LA level in order to establish the primary and secondary units of funding, which are then multiplied by October 2018 census data to produce final Schools Block allocations.

The DfE's file can be found by searching for 'NFF tables 2019 to 2020', or use the following link:

https://www.gov.uk/government/publications/national-funding-formula-tables-for-schools-and-high-needs-2019-to-2020.

The file you need is called 'Impact of the Schools NFF 2019-20'. You will need to click 'Enable Editing' to make the drop-down lists work. The file has a sheet labelled 'Look up a school'. You can select your LA area in cell E13 and then choose your school from the drop-down list at cell E15.

There are some caveats to the information that appears. Please bear in mind when working through our guidance that the allocations:

- relate to the <u>cumulative</u> impact of the NFF in the first two years;
- exclude premises, pupil mobility and growth;
- include lump sum and sparsity funding;
- do not cover funding outside of the NFF, such as Pupil Premium, sixth form funding, or SEN top up allocations;
- represent what the NFF calculation produces, which may not necessarily be what you will actually receive while funding is determined through local funding formulae;
- could change due to variations in pupil characteristics in future years or the DfE's decisions on formula values, depending on the settlement they receive from the Treasury from April 2020.

Despite these caveats, this analysis still provides a good indication of your overall trajectory towards the Hard NFF, especially when we know the majority of LAs are working towards the national values.

The file will show your school's illustrative formula results for 2019/20, excluding premises and pupil mobility factors. This was based on October 2017 rolls when the file was published in July 2018.

There is a lot of information here, but we don't need to look at it all. The cash figure and percentage change for 2019/20 have been overtaken by the actual results, now that October 2018 census data has been applied and LAs have taken their decisions on the formula.

The important piece of information is the last figure, in cell D44. This represents the percentage change in per-pupil funding for your school in the pure formula compared to your 2017/18 baseline. It should therefore be a reasonable guide for the longer-term trajectory.

The main difference between cell D44 and the percentage in cell D39 that is specific to 2019/20 is that in the pure formula (D44), capping hasn't been applied. However, it still includes the protections.

We will show you how to replicate this particular calculation for your 2019/20 actual funding compared to the same baseline of 2017/18. You can then compare this to the pure formula percentage and work out how much further your per-pupil funding is likely to change. Remember we will be adding other elements in separately at the end of the process.

Calculating your interim position in 2019/20

The vital question that will help you decide on the percentage change in per-pupil funding over the second and third year of the model is: what actually happened to your funding in 2019/20 and how does it compare to the ultimate pure formula percentage change?

This will act as a guide for the movement in your funding that you can safely assume for 2020/21 onwards. You may already know the answer to this question, but if you don't, we will now show you how to work out a like-for-like calculation, so you can compare it with the NFF illustrative allocations for the pure formula.

This method involves calculating the change in your per-pupil funding between 2017/18 (the original baseline for the NFF) and your actual 2019/20 allocation. All of the DfE's transitional calculations are based on this **two-year movement**, concluding the current Spending Review. This will form the basis for the next stage of the NFF.

This is a slightly different calculation to the one in the £ per pupil sheets of the model (which was based on the Minimum Funding Guarantee), because it excludes PFI and pupil mobility but includes the lump sum and sparsity factors. But for the purposes of our model, it's a good enough tool to estimate percentage changes for the majority of schools.

Find your budget statements for 2017/18 and 2019/20 and follow Activity 4 to achieve a meaningful comparison:

Activity 4: Calculating the pupil-led funding change between 2017/18 and 2019/20

- For each of the financial years 2017/18 and 2019/20, take your budget share/GAG and deduct the rates (LA schools only), PFI, split sites and pupil mobility factors (these are the historic spend factors which are excluded from the DfE's illustrative figures).
- Divide each year's total by the numbers of pupils on the relevant budget statement to represent per-pupil funding, i.e. the core NFF funding.
- Work out the difference between the per-pupil core NFF funding in 2017/18 and 2019/20 from the above calculations and express this as a percentage change.
- Compare this with the percentage change represented by the pure formula in cell D44 of the DfE's file.
- The PDF document shows an example; in this case, the school has a little further to go to reach the pure formula according to the DfE's calculation.

******

Here are some examples of possible scenarios that you might encounter, which will influence the future percentage changes that you choose for the second and third years of the model:

- The difference between the two percentages in the last bullet point of Activity 4 may be very close to the figure in cell D44 of the DfE's file. This means your LA decisions for 2019/20 have already put you close to the pure NFF (you may see this effect from an existing local formula). You won't see any further increase unless the 0.5% minimum increase continues from 2020/21 onwards, or your LA makes changes to the local formula which are beneficial to you, or the overall level of funding for schools improves as a result of the Spending Review.
- Your actual percentage difference for 2019/20 might be higher than the pure formula. This means that your local formula has been more beneficial than the NFF, either (for example) because the LA has retained the existing formula, or they are implementing the NFF but have been able to increase the amount available. In this situation, with the pure formula causing a reduction, you will probably trigger protection in years two and three of the model. How this plays out will depend on your LA's decisions in 2020/21, whether the Hard NFF is introduced or not in 2021/22, and what transitional arrangements are applied.
- Your actual percentage difference may be lower than the pure formula change. In this case, your LA may not have moved towards the NFF, or if it is progressing towards it, the arrangements for transition (protection and capping) may be different from the government's assumptions in the calculation of the LA's DSG. The rate at which you move towards the pure formula result will depend on your LA's decisions in 2020/21, whether the Hard NFF is introduced or not in 2021/22, and what transitional arrangements are applied.

There are some overarching principles which you can refer to in any of these situations, as you consider which percentages to use for years two and three of the model.

When we talk about transitional arrangements and protection, remember that under the current regulations, your local authority cannot reduce your funding by more than 1.5% per pupil per year, as that is the statutory Minimum Funding Guarantee protection.

For schools with very low additional needs, the NFF provides an additional layer of protection: the Minimum Funding Level (MFL). LAs are not obliged to apply this protection in the local formula. If they do implement it, schools that are eligible must not have their gains capped. This can lead to high increases in funding above the capping level. If your LA has not implemented the MFL, you could see a big gap between your 2019/20 result and the pure formula in the DfE's file.

Your actual funding in 2020/21, and in 2021/22 if local formulae are still in place, depends on:

a) whether your LA is moving towards the NFF or not;
b) whether the local formula produces a gain or a loss for you;
c) if your formula result is a loss, the level of protection selected by the LA;
d) if your formula result is a gain, whether the LA uses capping or not, and if it does, what capping level is chosen.

It can be tricky to anticipate LA decisions, because they depend on the amount of funding received and changes in data. There is a time lag between the data used to calculate the primary and secondary per-pupil units of funding within DSG and the data that has to be used to distribute funding through the formula. LAs have to manage this by considering whether to change formula values for particular factors.

Another common issue, which is due to population growth, is that LAs have to provide funding for new cohorts in new and growing schools from the formula pot, in advance of being given grant for it.

Nevertheless, we have to make some assumptions in order to make the model robust. The process we have outlined above provides definitive data on which to base your assumptions, which is far better than hazarding a guess.

As we've already outlined, the process of presenting alternative scenarios will make it much easier for stakeholders to accept that there can be an acceptable margin of error in your forecasting. The DfE does not expect your multi-year budgets to be 100% accurate; it is much more about taking a strategic high-level view to inform your forward planning.

Principles to consider

While the above information should provide a good indication of the percentage change you can apply to years two and three in the model, you need to weigh up all the different information based on what's happening in your local area and make your own decisions.

There are four main questions to consider, using all the information we have provided up to this point:

- What does the pure NFF for your school look like, compared to where you are now?
- What is your LA's strategy: to move towards the NFF or not?
- How long is it likely to take for you to reach the pure formula?
- What assumption do you want to make about the timing of the Hard NFF?

Working through these questions will help you reach a decision on the percentage changes needed in the model. Once you reach the pure formula, your per-pupil funding will only increase if there is a continuing positive percentage figure for the Minimum Funding Guarantee, or if either the government or your LA makes more funding available.

It is better to be prudent than over-optimistic. Given the scope for local decisions in 2020/21 and possibly 2021/22 if primary legislation isn't passed to achieve a Hard NFF by then, you may consider using the MFG rate of -1.5% for your worst-case option in both years.

This holds true even if you know there is a large positive gap between your 2019/20 percentage change and the pure formula change. You can reflect the potential for an increase in your best-case option, and exercise judgement somewhere between the two in the middle-case option for a more realistic position.

We advise you to keep an eye on communications from the DfE as the Spending Review progresses. As further information becomes available, you can return to the model and change the percentages very easily. The best way of keeping up to date is to sign up for our newsletter at https://schoolfinancialsuccess.com to receive a monthly update with key government announcements on school funding.

To keep informed about key discussions in relation to the local formula, you can look at your local Schools Forum website, where you should find reports and minutes of meetings. Why not raise an agenda item at your network meetings so that Schools Forum members can maintain a dialogue about the coming year's budget strategy with those they are representing?

Recording percentage changes for per-pupil funding

Once you have decided what makes sense for your school's options, it's time to put it into the model and then move on to the next stage, roll projections. It may feel like a momentous decision, because you've had to go through quite a lengthy process to consider all the influencing factors, but nothing is set in stone. The model is designed to be flexible.

After you've gone through the full process, you can review the final three scenarios for the overall model, and if there isn't enough of a difference between them to generate a useful debate, you can come back to these percentages and tweak them.

Try to keep a proportionate view of the choices across the best, middle and worst-case options. You may feel that there is a relatively small range of possibilities for the changes in per-pupil funding, and this is true: the initial phase of the NFF produces potential changes between -1.5% and +3% per year.

But this is only half of your forecasting model. You will be blending the funding aspect with roll projections, which is when the differences between the combined scenarios really starts to become apparent.

Keep the end view in mind. The purpose of a worst-case option is to show SLT and governors the lowest possible level of funding, to stimulate their thinking about how the school would respond. The best-case option will prompt ideas on how you might use any increase to cover cost pressures in particular areas, or even invest it in improvement strategies. The middle-case option is meant to be the most realistic forecast.

Now you can return to your model and put the thinking you've just done into practice, by populating the three £ per pupil sheets with the relevant percentage changes.

Activity 5: Populating the £ per pupil percentage changes

- Review the suggestions for your category in this chapter. Are there any other local circumstances which could affect your funding, especially if your LA isn't working towards the NFF?
- Enter the percentage changes in per-pupil funding across the three years in the best, middle and worst-case sheets of the model.
- Check that the calculation produces the correct result in each column.
- Our PDF contains a fictitious example of a Best £ per pupil calculation for a primary school; we will use this as our example throughout the book for you to refer to.

******

Conclusions - £ per pupil changes

We've already talked about the forecasts being broad-brush and high-level, so don't tie yourself in knots trying to decide on an exact percentage change for each per-pupil funding option across the three years. Use your natural instincts, along with the information we provided, to assess what the government's and/or your LA's approaches might mean for your funding levels.

Ultimately, the task involves assessing your starting point in relation to the NFF values, then identifying whether your LA is moving the local formula towards them or not, and guessing (frankly) when the Hard NFF is likely to be introduced. You are trying to get a sensible set of options that move from the highest to the lowest possible outcomes across the multi-year period.

Now we'll move on to the second part of the equation, how to construct best, middle and worst-case options for your future rolls.

7   ROLL PROJECTIONS

The impact of changing rolls

Having identified the potential changes in the amount of funding per pupil that your school is likely to receive under the new funding system, the next element you need to consider is your future pupil numbers.

A full school with stable pupil numbers is the ideal situation for any school, making forward planning much easier. However, many schools have to manage a more volatile situation.

Significant and persistent reductions in pupil numbers can be catastrophic for a school. Premises-related costs, especially energy, tend not to reduce at the same pace as the downturn in pupils. If a PFI contract is in existence, it can severely limit a school's flexibility to reduce costs.

Staffing costs can be reviewed in response to lower numbers, but it takes time to realise savings. Often, it's not possible to achieve a reduction directly in proportion to changing rolls, because of the need for optimum class sizes to suit the needs of the pupils. This is a particularly challenging problem with subject options in secondary schools - somehow surplus teaching capacity never happens in the right place to match the ideal plan for altering the curriculum.

Changes in the structure have to be carefully planned and thought out to avoid unnecessarily high staff turnover, a potential recruitment crisis or instability in staffing. It's possible to cut staffing, only to be caught out by an unexpected increase in rolls in subsequent years.

Small schools can find it especially difficult to cope with changes in pupil numbers. They tend to rely on the lump sum, and the sparsity factor for those in rural areas, to provide some stability.

However, the NFF has created the potential for change in these values. Historically, some authorities have had a much higher lump sum in their local formulae (up to the maximum permitted level of £175,000) and the rate may have varied between primary and secondary schools. However, the NFF rate is only £110,000 for both phases. Some LAs have retained this higher value or reduced it only slightly while they still have the option. But ultimately, the Hard NFF will impose the lower rate for all schools.

The situation is similar for sparsity. However, some schools might benefit from this; some LAs did not use the factor even if they had some rural schools, but the NFF awards it to all eligible schools.

High pupil mobility, where pupils frequently move in and out of individual schools during an academic year, can be a critical issue for some schools. They find it very difficult to predict how many pupils will be on roll at any point, and census day becomes crucial. Pupil mobility can have an adverse impact on funding, strategic planning and ultimately pupil outcomes.

While the DfE agreed to retain the pupil mobility factor when it finalised the NFF, it is currently funded on a historic spend basis. An initial attempt was made to explore how it could be brought into the NFF with a formulaic approach, but there was insufficient confidence in the data and the threshold that should be used. It has therefore remained as a historic spend factor for 2019/20.

It is therefore up to LAs to decide how to treat it in the local formula, which will usually by governed by the October census data outcomes. Even if a factor exists (not all LAs use it), all schools have to absorb the first 10% of mobility and payment is only for new pupils above the 10%.

The result of these changes is that pure pupil numbers are even more vital to your funding.

Using estimates of future rolls within the model will help to improve your financial planning in times of pupil roll uncertainty. When you present the forecasts to other leaders and governors, you will need to underline the fact that you can't be precise, and they should expect some variations when actual pupils materialise.

The use of scenarios helps to illustrate this, by allowing for a range of possibilities to be tested; highlighting the difference between relatively low pupil number variations once they are combined with per-pupil funding can open everyone's eyes to the potential for turbulence in future allocations of funding.

Setting up the roll projections worksheet

Unlike the £ per pupil worksheets, you only need to create one worksheet to cover all three options for roll projections. We've constructed an example, but you don't need to follow it; do whatever meets your needs.

Your aim at this stage of the model is to produce best, middle and worst-case options for the pupil numbers that will drive your funding for the next three years. You will want to allow for any known trends, e.g. if you have a particular pattern of changes in cohort size as they move up the school, or if there is an unusual transition point at which pupils might move to another school (such as a middle school in a neighbouring area instead of a local secondary school). We suggest the use of a turnover allowance applied to the rolls as groups move up each year, but you might not need to use this.

Always consider our suggestions in the light of your own circumstances. Keep in mind your aim, which is to produce a total roll for each option for the three-year period. Always remember you should be focusing on the **funded** rolls for the current year (i.e. the October prior to the start of each financial year, not the actual pupils you are teaching during that academic year).

Activity 6: Creating the roll projections sheet

- Add a blank worksheet to the file after the Worst £ per pupil sheet and name the tab 'Roll projections'. Follow our suggested layout if you find it helpful:

	A	B	C	D	E	F	G	H	I	J
1	**Roll projections - Best, Middle & Worst Case Scenarios**									
2	Tailor this sheet to your own year groups									
3										
4	1. Roll projections - best case option									
5			R	Y1	Y2	Y3	Y4	Y5	Y6	R-Y6 total
6										
7	Oct-18	2019/20	51	52	50	44	38	42	44	321
8	Oct-19	2020/21								-
9	Oct-20	2021/22								-
10										
11	Turnover allowance									
12										
13	2. Roll projections - middle case option									
14			R	Y1	Y2	Y3	Y4	Y5	Y6	R-Y6 total
15										
16	Oct-18	2019/20	51	52	50	44	38	42	44	321
17	Oct-19	2020/21								-
18	Oct-20	2021/22								-
19										
20	Turnover allowance									
21										
22	3. Roll projections - worst case option									
23			R	Y1	Y2	Y3	Y4	Y5	Y6	R-Y6 total
24										
25	Oct-18	2019/20	51	52	50	44	38	42	44	321
26	Oct-19	2020/21								-
27	Oct-20	2021/22								-
28										
29	Turnover allowance									

- Create a title: 1. Roll projections - best-case option.
- Create row labels for the census points of October 2018, 2019 and 2020 in the first column and the corresponding financial years 2019/20 through to 2021/22 in the second column. As already noted, you will be working with the pupil data that drives your funding (i.e. lagged data), not the pupils on which your curriculum and staffing plans are based.
- Create column headings for the year groups relevant to your school and a total column at the end. Tailor this if you have a structure that cuts across primary and secondary phases.
- If required, add a turnover allowance row, formatted as a percentage, to adjust year groups that don't move on intact. You can ignore this if you have consistently stable rolls or if you plan to enter rolls manually. If you're not sure, we recommend you incorporate the row while you are focusing on the model development. You can always reconsider later on and ignore this row if it isn't needed.

- Copy the table and paste it twice below the first section, labelling the new sections 2 and 3 for the other two options.
- You can shade cells in different colours to differentiate between data entry cells and those with formulae.
- Enter the October 2018 FTE pupil census data across the year groups in the row for 2019/20 (row 7 in our example).
- These are actuals, so they won't change for the middle and worst-case options. You can copy and paste them into rows 16 and 25, or you can create a formula to pick up the figure from row 7 in the other two options.
- Sum the year group cells in column J for each year.
- Format the cells in each of the data rows as whole numbers and the turnover allowance cells as a percentage.
- The remaining cells will be calculated in our next activity, using a formula to move the year groups forward each year.

******

Progressing the year groups

Your actual funded pupils in 2019/20 (those on roll at October 2018) will be used as a baseline. This will allow you to roll forward year groups for the following two years before estimating admissions for your intake year.

Activity

Activity 7: Calculating the progression of year groups

- For each of the three options, you can either enter roll estimates directly, or create a formula to transfer each year group to the following year, e.g. cell D8 would read =C7.
- If you wish to build a turnover allowance into the model, amend the formula to take it into account. Starting with cell D8, change the formula to the following: =C7*(1+D11) to apply the turnover allowance. You can use the ROUND function with a 0 at the end of the formula to create whole numbers if you wish.

You can ignore the turnover allowance if you are absolutely confident that it isn't necessary, or if you intend to enter the pupil numbers directly into the cells.

- Copy and paste (or drag) the formula to the other year group cells in the same row (E8:I8). The set of year group cells can then be copied down (or selected and dragged) into cells D9:I9.
- Repeat the process for the middle and worst-case options.
- We suggest you set your turnover allowance to 0% initially, so you can easily check that each year group is moving on to the next in a subsequent year. Then enter any percentages as required (positive or negative) to see the difference they make.
- Our PDF contains the formulae we used for this activity. It includes some figures entered in the new intake year column, to make the references clearer. But you don't need to enter any rolls in the new intake year column yet, as we will be providing some information to help you decide on those. Your turnover allowance row can also stay blank for now.

******

Best, middle and worst-case options

So far, you have focused on setting up the options in your model. We will be providing some guidance in the next chapter on the issues you need to consider when attempting to predict future rolls. But first we want to explain your options for using this worksheet, so you can bear them in mind as you start to develop the different options for your future pupil numbers.

There are two methods for creating differences between the best, middle and worst-case options. Firstly, you can enter different estimates for your intake years, which will flow through as they move through the three-year period. In addition, you can use the turnover allowance row for each option, entering a positive or negative change to reflect changes in individual year groups in each census. The combination of these two gives you a more flexible set of forecasts.

The turnover allowance can be a standard percentage across all year groups within an option, or it can be varied. This is useful if you have some year groups which are more volatile than others. A good example is if you are in a two-tier system, but a neighbouring authority or some local academies could operate a three-tier system. The impact could be that local community or other academy primary schools might lose pupils before Y6 as they transfer to a middle school, or secondary schools could see transfers to a high school within KS3.

If you want a different turnover allowance for each of years two and three, rather than the same percentage, just add another allowance row and reference that in your year three formula.

We've emphasised that the figures in each of the years relate to the funded rolls i.e. in the October prior to the financial year under consideration. This lagged system buys you some time if you are experiencing falling rolls, but in a rising rolls situation it means the growth has to be funded from the school's existing resources until the next financial year, unless it's an expansion agreed with the LA. For LA schools, the pressure is for two terms and for academies it is three terms (unless the funding agreement specifies estimated rolls).

You've now completed the set-up of your roll projections sheet and have entered your baseline figures. The next chapter will help you think about how to populate the intake year and the turnover allowances for each of the options across the three-year period.

8 DEVELOPING ASSUMPTIONS: FUTURE ROLLS

Influences on your future rolls

This chapter will consider the potential reasons for changes in pupil numbers. It will also suggest how you can use the available information and your own local knowledge to decide on the most appropriate level of new admissions and any turnover allowance for the best, middle and worst-case options. Like the £ per pupil elements of the model, this will have a big influence on the final scenarios you produce, so it needs careful thought.

In relation to forecasting future pupil numbers, your local knowledge is invaluable. There are many reasons why a school's roll can go up or down, and not all of them can be predicted. We will now set out our top tips for areas to explore, in no particular order.

1. Relationships with the community

Do you have a good relationship with those who currently care for your prospective pupils or who can influence their future choices? It's an important consideration when trying to maximise admissions.

For primary schools, this will include parents and carers of existing pupils (especially if they already have younger children), early years settings including private providers, childminders and playgroups, and any community groups where parents and carers gather.

Secondary schools will see primary schools as important, not only those with whom there are formal admission links, but potentially any around the local area. Schools that are further afield can be considered if transport links and parental preferences indicate that there is some interest.

Don't forget grandparents; many help to care for their grandchildren on a regular basis and they may play a big part in the choice of school. They might have allegiances to a different school, perhaps another which is nearer to them.

Do you let the community access your school, for example at special events, or by letting space to groups for their leisure activities? This is a good way of showing them the facilities on offer and making local people feel part of the school. It can also bring in income, as long as you get the balance right and avoid overcharging.

2. <u>Competition from other schools</u>

What does the competition look like for admissions in your area? This will partly be a matter of distance, depending on the ability and willingness of parents to travel.

Have other schools been particularly aggressive in their marketing to potential pupils, or fostered stronger relationships with nursery settings or schools in the area whose pupils normally transfer to you?

Do others offer something that you don't, e.g. a more attractive curriculum choice, childcare, a greater variety of after school clubs, better links with the community, or particular strengths in technology, sport, music, performing arts and so on?

Has a Free School opened in your area, or have existing schools and academies expanded, which in some cases can cause over-capacity?

Don't assume that all schools will be adversarial about admissions. You may be able to identify a group of headteachers and principals who can see the benefits of working together across an area to prevent the loss of pupils to schools in another locality. While this often happens naturally in multi-academy trusts, it can work with any group of schools.

3. <u>Changes in leadership</u>

Have you had leadership changes recently, and have parents and carers responded positively or negatively? Sometimes it can only take a difference of opinion with a couple of parents to cause problems, whatever the issue (and it can seem a very small issue to you).

If you are a new headteacher, have you made sure you are visible to families, community leaders and influencers? Have you articulated your vision for the school clearly to everyone who might encourage or discourage potential pupils and their families? Never underestimate the power of who you know as well as what you know.

4. Inspection judgements

Have you been inspected recently, and how have parents reacted to the report? How did you handle the publicity?

If it was a good result, did you pay enough attention to letting everyone know about your success? If it was an adverse outcome, did you send consistent and confident messages about how you were going to put things right?

A lot depends on the timing of the report's publication, but depending on the factors your prospective parents consider, it can have a significant impact on applications for places.

5. Pupil outcomes

Can you identify any obvious correlation between test and examination results and trends in admissions and retention of pupils?

How do you handle the announcement of your pupils' achievements? Do you celebrate all types of success, not just those with the highest levels, grades or progress? Do you present a fair and accurate picture?

Some parents place more importance on non-academic outcomes and rely on gut instinct when visiting a school. You might be surprised at the number who don't even try to find out the results for the schools they are considering. Young people place great emphasis on being with their friends. A dip in results might not have the detrimental impact that you fear; you can reflect this through the different options in the model.

6. Housing changes

Have there been any recent new housing developments, redevelopment of an area, or clearance of old houses in the locality from which you take pupils? Are there any plans for developments in the future?

Changes in the provision of housing can not only affect the number of children and young people in your area, but also their profile.

It is notoriously difficult to predict the impact of a new housing estate on the number of children in your target area for admissions, even if the houses appear to be of a type to attract families. Often a proportion will move within an area, rather than coming new to it. If families in this position have easy access to transport, their children may remain in their current school.

Your local authority will publish plans for new housing, although it's often very difficult to be precise about timescales. But it's certainly worth watching out for information, or indeed asking for it.

7. In-year pupil turnover

Does your school experience high pupil mobility, i.e. a random pattern of starters and leavers throughout the year? There are many different reasons for this. Some parents who do not initially get the school of their choice may decide to move their child if a place later becomes available. Service families will move due to a new posting. Other cases involve multiple moves, sometimes associated with deprivation. Depending on the reason, it's not always easy to influence the movement of pupils.

Are some year groups more prone to change than others? We've already mentioned that this can be a particular issue if you have a neighbouring area that operates a different tiered system to your LA.

Do you serve an area with high levels of international new arrivals? This is another complex area, and it can go hand-in-hand with higher levels of English as an Additional Language. Central government has programmes in some LAs to house refugees and asylum seekers. The locations are often chosen because there are high numbers of low-cost rented properties, which also generate changes of school for other reasons: seasonal workers, families rehoused because of poor conditions, evictions for rent arrears, or non-payers vanishing to escape debt.

If you have high pupil mobility, it's worth giving some thought to what the reasons are, and whether you can exercise any influence in parents' decisions about a move. You might join with other schools in a similar situation in an attempt to create a different ethos among parents, by highlighting the detrimental impact it can sometimes have on a child's education.

The amount of work it takes to admit, settle in and assess a new starter at any other times than the normal point, and the fact that funding often isn't sufficient, will act as a motivator to try to reduce mobility wherever possible.

8. Press coverage

Do you have good relationships with the local press? Often minor incidents will cast a disproportionate shadow over a school: a parent with an unjustified grudge against a member of staff, residents being upset by the behaviour of some pupils who pass by their properties, pupils forgetting they are ambassadors for the school when visible in uniform and so on.

One careless sentence quoted by a journalist, or a misrepresentation of what you said, can elicit a strong reaction from the public and put off prospective parents. You can be proactive by building relationships with the local media to promote positive messages. Sometimes staff in the LA's press office can be useful allies.

Analysing previous pupil number trends

It's worth spending a little time analysing recent trends in pupil numbers, looking backwards before you start the process of considering future rolls. By doing this, you may be able to identify a pattern related to particular events or local circumstances.

The next activity asks you to think through the eight influencing factors we've just outlined and consider whether they are relevant to your situation. Feel free to add any others that are relevant to your situation.

Activity 8: Analysing previous pupil number trends

- Look at your October census results for the last three to five years and identify any obvious patterns, both in admissions and in the way year groups progress through the school.
- Can you make connections between these patterns and any of the areas we discussed earlier? Here they are again:
    1. Relationships with the community
    2. Competition from other schools
    3. Changes in leadership
    4. Inspection judgements
    5. Pupil outcomes
    6. Housing changes
    7. In-year pupil turnover
    8. Press coverage
- Have you kept any of your LA's pupil projection information from these years? Were they accurate? Were there particular reasons why any predicted increase or deterioration in numbers didn't materialise?
- Make notes on your observations and refer to them while considering how pupil numbers might change in the future.

*****

Looking ahead - sources of information

Besides your own records and local knowledge, there are some other sources of information which can help you in estimating what your future rolls might look like.

Those responsible for school organisation at the local authority are valuable contacts, since they will have an overview of population changes and the pattern of need for places at a locality level. The LA is responsible for place planning across all types of school, even where some schools in the area are their own admissions authorities. Academies have as much right as LA schools to ask for information. How you use the intelligence is your responsibility.

Local authorities have a statutory duty to achieve sufficiency of places. They understand all the statistical information about birth rates, housing yields, and cross-boundary movement between schools, and should be happy to share information and work with you to ensure demand can be met.

Councils with education responsibilities usually provide pupil number predictions at locality level to help schools with their forward planning. This can be a challenging task and accuracy rates can vary. It involves taking a lot of different perspectives into account, starting with national data on population projections from the Office for National Statistics. You can find the latest projections up to 2025, which were published in July 2018, at the following link:

https://www.gov.uk/government/statistics/national-pupil-projections-july-2018

Here is an extract from the summary report:

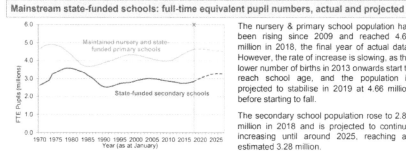

Mainstream state-funded schools: full-time equivalent pupil numbers, actual and projected

The nursery & primary school population has been rising since 2009 and reached 4.64 million in 2018, the final year of actual data. However, the rate of increase is slowing, as the lower number of births in 2013 onwards start to reach school age, and the population is projected to stabilise in 2019 at 4.66 million before starting to fall.

The secondary school population rose to 2.85 million in 2018 and is projected to continue increasing until around 2025, reaching an estimated 3.28 million.

This report identifies a change in data since last year's publication which demonstrates that pupil projections are not an easy task, even at national level:

'In 2017 we were projecting an increase of around 102,000 in the primary and nursery school population over the projection period, to 4.68 million by 2026. This year, however, the projection estimates there will be a decrease of 112,000 between 2018 and 2027, to 4.52 million. This is because of lower projected births which then feed into lower numbers starting school.'.

If this can happen at the highest level of projections, you can see how challenging it is for local authorities to be accurate when trying to assess the trends at area-wide, locality, and individual school levels.

Parental preference operates in some strange and unpredictable ways at times. But it is worth bearing the LA forecasts in mind, and exploring further the features that they have built into the model. They may suggest some changes in local population patterns that you weren't aware of.

If you couldn't do the last part of Activity 8 because you didn't have the information on LA pupil projections, it's worth starting to retain these predictions. In subsequent years, you can then compare them to what actually happened and try to identify reasons for the difference.

Were there any unexpected events or circumstances that caused it? Or is there a fundamental problem with the accuracy of the predictions? We are referring to the highest level predictions, because of the difficulties in forecasting long-term individual school rolls.

If you suspect the high-level prediction model is at fault, it is worth asking to speak to the local authority's school organisation expert to let them know of your concerns. They will usually welcome the feedback and be keen to work with you to find out what went wrong. Whether this provides answers or not, you will need to bear in mind any inaccuracies in the predictions when moving to the next stage of considering what might happen to your rolls in the future.

Similarly, the Admissions team will have a sense of trends in parental preference. Admissions Forums are no longer part of the statutory landscape, but the LA should be reporting facts to headteachers through alternative mechanisms such as headteacher and governor briefings. These should include parental preference data and the proportion of preferences that were met. This will tell you a lot about which are the most popular schools, as well as details of the movement in pupil numbers, in-year transfers and whether patterns are changing.

If this communication isn't happening, talk to your Schools Forum representative or a headteacher who is on one of the LA groups that give access to senior officers, and ask them to raise it.

As we said at the beginning of this chapter, your local knowledge can be more influential than national or local information, but the best approach is to try to blend the two.

Having a range of best, middle and worst-case options will allow you to demonstrate the level of uncertainty and show a range of possibilities. This is another area where it's crucial to make clear to your leadership team and governors that there will inevitably be a margin of error.

Forecasting future rolls

Now we come to the crux of the matter: your assessment of potential future changes in pupil numbers at your school. By using this model, you are being proactive and giving your school a much better chance of achieving informed funding projections.

Pupil numbers can have a significant impact on your funding, making the difference between a sustainable budget and a financial crisis. How likely is it that the past trends you have identified will continue?

You may already have financial planning software with roll forecasts in it. How long ago did you prepare them? What assumptions did you make? Are they up to date? Now is a good time to review them and consider whether circumstances have changed. Are there different influences on your pupil numbers now, compared to a couple of years ago?

This is not an exact science, and a lot of it will be based on intelligence gathered from a range of sources, some of which we've already highlighted. It also needs a large slice of your own judgement. There are many uncertainties, but just as we have done in the per-pupil funding question, it is better to consider the possibilities and prepare for them than to shrug your shoulders and say you can't do anything because it's impossible to tell what might happen.

Your starting point therefore is to look at your list of past trends and consider if or how they might apply in the future. Which areas are within your control and which are you unable to influence? Focusing on the aspects that you can do something about will help you feel more positive about your future forecasts.

Next, consider what actions you could take to reduce the risks that you've identified. These may be linked to the eight influences we discussed earlier, or you could find some others, depending on your circumstances.

You will probably come up with a lot of questions, but you aren't expected to have all the answers - there are so many unknown factors. The point is that awareness of all these issues and spending time discussing them with colleagues will give you a far better chance of making reasonable predictions for the future.

These are only suggestions as a starting point; you will know your own circumstances and can judge what the main issues are that you need to look at. Talk to as many people as you can to elicit information and opinions about what the future holds.

Arrange a discussion with your governing body about the patterns you have identified and your thoughts on what might change in the future. Your school may be lucky enough to have governors with their finger on the pulse of the community or who are part of organisations involved in driving some of the changes you've identified, and they may be able to provide further information to add to the mix.

Education is such a fast-changing world that you can't possibly be expected to know everything. Making connections with people who know a lot about a small aspect is vital - then you can piece together the available information and start to make some sense of it all. Place planning is a good example of this.

It is your call as to how much weight you attach to each piece of information. Be sure to ask the following questions before evaluating it as a basis for your assumptions: is it evidenced, reasonably reliable, and likely to have relevance to the number of children who may come to your school in the future?

Make sure you record your assumptions and the rationale for your choices. This will help you to follow the logic you have used when you return to your projections at a later date to review them for a rolled-forward version of your multi-year budget forecast. Understanding the elements within the projections means you can test them against what actually happened, and refine your planning going forward.

Your projections and the assumptions behind them can be shared with governors, demonstrating you are taking forward planning seriously by building forecasts of future rolls into your financial strategy. Our approach includes a School Financial Sustainability Plan as a summary of your work; by recording your assumptions as you go through the process, this will more or less write itself.

The governing body needs to be part of the forward planning process; Ofsted will expect to see their involvement at a strategic level. When there are any leadership changes, it is essential that a new headteacher or Chair of Governors can pick up the projections and quickly get an understanding of the assumptions and the basis on which they have been made.

The next activity is to complete the roll projections by entering estimated intakes and turnover allowances if applicable. You may prefer to enter all of the roll projections directly into the model, in which case you can ignore the instructions.

Activity 9: Completing roll projections

- Use all the available information to estimate your intake for the next three years under the best, middle and worst-case options.
- Enter these estimates into the intake year column against each year (Reception column in our example).
- If you believe that some of your year groups are not likely to progress intact or could increase, enter appropriate turnover allowances in the relevant row for each option.
- Consider whether the turnover allowances for each year group are likely to vary between the best, middle and worst-case options. It's a way of adding more sensitivity to your forecasts. You can insert a separate turnover allowance row in each option if you want different rates for 2020/21 and 2021/22.
- Consult the completed example in the PDF document if you want to see how we approached the activity.

******

You'll be glad to hear that you've now completed the bulk of the work needed to create the basis of your forecasts. The two key elements, the amount per pupil and future rolls, are now in place within the model for your three options across the next three years. You can come back to them if further information becomes available and you want to adjust any of the figures.

The next stage is to put these two elements together, to create all nine possible combinations. Our next chapter shows you how to do this, so that you are ready to narrow down the nine potential combinations to just three for further development as full scenarios.

9 COMBINING YOUR PROJECTIONS

The power of combinations

So far, we have considered the two main elements of your funding separately: the amount per pupil and the number of pupils. You can see the progression of your per-pupil funding as you change the percentages across the years for the three different options. The roll projections table clearly shows the impact of different admissions and pupil mobility on your total figures.

But it's when you start to put together the two elements that you start to see how powerful the interaction is between them. Let's take just one example, so you can start to see the impact of changing rolls on funding. Using our fictitious primary school's average baseline per pupil of £3,824.17 for 2019/20, let's see what happens with the roll changes between best and worst-case scenarios.

	Best	Worst	Difference	Baseline value change
2019/20	321	321	-	-
2020/21	326	305	-21	-£80,308
2021/22	330	291	-39	-£149,143

This example is based on a static per-pupil value, so you can imagine how rapidly this will change when you have different funding values between the best and worst-case scenarios.

As you bring together the funding and rolls options, consider whether they are producing figures with a reasonable differential between them. You are trying to identify shades of possibilities in the two different elements, and you'll then put them together. You won't want to spend time debating fairly marginal variations. As you will see in a moment, there are nine possible combinations.

Later on, you will need to decide which three out of the nine combinations should be developed into full scenarios. Thinking about your confidence levels in either per-pupil funding or your future pupil numbers as you go through this process will help you in choosing your final three scenarios.

Mapping the combinations

Your next activity involves calculating all the combinations of your best, middle and worst-case per pupil funding and roll projections to identify the full range of funding possibilities. You will be mapping them against each other to produce nine possible combinations, as shown in the following table.

	Best £ per pupil	Middle £ per pupil	Worst £ per pupil
Best roll	1	4	7
Middle roll	2	5	8
Worst roll	3	6	9

Activity

Activity 10: Setting up the Combinations worksheet

- Add a blank worksheet to the file after the Roll Projections sheet and name it Combinations.
- Create fields as shown in the blank example on the next page. This is the first section, which combines your best £ per pupil figures with the best, middle and worst-case options for your rolls across the three years.
- This will enable you to create scenarios 1 to 3 in the table shown above this activity.

	A	B	C	D
1	**Combinations of per pupil funding and roll projections**			
2				
3	Do not change any fields - all are referenced from other sheets and calculated automatically			
4				
5		2019/20	2020/21	2021/22
6	**Best case £ per pupil funding**			
7				
8	1. **Best case rolls**			
9	Pupil-led funding total			
10	Plus MFG exclusions			
11		£ -	£ -	£ -
12				
13	2. **Middle case rolls**			
14	Pupil-led funding total			
15	Plus MFG exclusions			
16		£ -	£ -	£ -
17				
18	3. **Worst case rolls**			
19	Pupil-led funding total			
20	Plus MFG exclusions			
21		£ -	£ -	£ -

- Create a formula for each of the scenarios 1 to 3 (in rows 11, 16 and 21) which adds together the figures in the two rows labelled 'Pupil-led funding total' and 'Plus MFG exclusions' (lines 9 and 10 for scenario 1).
- We found it helpful to shade the Best case £ per pupil funding cells and the row cells in separate colours (see our PDF), as a reminder that you are going to apply the figures in the top row to the three options for rolls for scenarios 1 to 3.
- Now copy and paste this whole section twice underneath, changing the 'Best' descriptor in 'Best case £ per pupil funding' to 'Middle' and 'Worst' for the two new sections. You will also need to renumber the scenarios, from 4 to 6 for the three roll options under the Middle case £ per pupil funding heading, and from 7 to 9 for the three roll options within the Worst case £ per pupil funding heading. If in doubt, refer to the table just before this activity and check our PDF document.

******

You are now ready to populate the combinations worksheet. There is no need for any data entry work in this sheet, because the relevant information is already in your three £ per pupil sheets and the roll projections sheet. It's simply a matter of creating the right formulae to transfer the existing figures from the other sheets. You must make absolutely sure that you are picking up the correct cells.

It's helpful to put a reminder at the top of the sheet that no data should be entered, to guard against accidental overwriting, but you can also lock the cells and protect the sheet when you are confident that your formulae are all accurate.

Our first task is to populate the best, middle and worst-case £ per pupil options in this worksheet (Activity 11). We found it easiest to create the figures in these three items first. The second task is to populate the three roll options under each one (Activity 12).

Then we can multiply each of the options with the others to produce the pupil-led funding total for each of the nine possible combinations (Activity 13), before adding back the items we excluded right at the start of the exercise (Activity 14).

Activity 11: Combinations: populating £ per pupil funding

- Working only on the 'Best case £ per pupil funding' row at the top of the Combinations sheet (row 6 in our PDF example):
  - In the cell below the heading for 2019/20 (cell B6), create a formula to reference the 2019/20 baseline per-pupil funding from your Best £ per pupil worksheet. You'll find this in cell C13 in our PDF Activity 5 completed example. This row reference only applies to the baseline year - you'll recall that the other two years have extra steps.
  - On the same 'Best case £ per pupil funding' row, in the next column (cell C6), create a formula to reference the 2020/21 MFG protected value per pupil from the Best £ per pupil worksheet. This is in cell D16 in our PDF Activity 5 completed example, i.e. the adjusted value after you have applied a percentage change. Note that you can't copy this

from the cell for 2019/20, as we are referencing a different row for 2020/21.

  o Copy and paste cell C6 (or drag the right-hand lower corner) into cell D6 for 2021/22 to pick up the correct per pupil funding amount from the Best £ per pupil worksheet. If you are following our example, it should refer to cell E16 in that worksheet.

- Repeat the above process for the 'Middle case £ per pupil funding' values (row 24 in the PDF example) but referencing the items from the Middle £ per pupil worksheet.
- Do the same for the 'Worst case £ per pupil funding' values (row 42 in the PDF example) but referencing the items from the Worst £ per pupil worksheet.

This sets the three different £ per pupil options. Make sure the figures are correct before moving on.

Step 2 is to populate the best, middle and worst-case rolls fields.

Activity

Activity 12: Combinations: populating rolls

- In the Combinations worksheet, start with the first roll option within the 'Best case per pupil funding' section. This is labelled '1. Best case rolls', row 8 in our example.
- Enter a formula to pick up the total rolls cell from the section of your Roll projections worksheet labelled '1. Roll projections - best case scenario' (cell J7 for 2019/20 in our PDF in Activity 9, cell J8 for 2019/20 and so on). Our example only shows primary rolls; you will need to choose the correct column reference for your overall total if you have a different age range.
  As you enter each formula, press the F4 key once to fix the reference (column and row). This will speed up the process once you've done the first set of three roll options.
- You will be entering formulae across a row in the Combinations worksheet, but referencing figures working down the column in

the roll projections worksheet. So be careful to check that you are picking up the correct figures.

- Repeat this for the second roll option which is labelled '2. Middle case rolls' (row 13 in our example), still within the 'Best per pupil funding' set of options in the Combinations sheet. This time you will be referencing the total rolls from the 'Roll projections - middle case scenario' section of the roll projections worksheet (J16, J17 and J18). Fix the references again using F4.

- Repeat for the third roll option labelled '3. Worst case rolls' (row 18 in our example), still within the 'Best per pupil funding' set of options in the Combinations sheet. You will pick up J25, J26 and J27 from the roll projections. Fix the references again using F4.

- Now for the short cut. Because you've fixed the references, you can copy each of the rows of roll forecasts into the same option's row in the middle and worst per pupil funding sections. The completed cells for '1. Best case rolls' can be copied into scenarios 4 and 7. The cells for '2. Middle case rolls' can be copied to scenarios 5 and 8, and cells for '3. Worst case rolls' can go in scenarios 6 and 9.

******

Step 3 is to start multiplying the two elements together to produce the nine potential combinations.

Activity 13: Combinations: calculating pupil-led funding totals

- For each set of combinations, you will be now be working on the row labelled 'Pupil-led funding total'. You'll be starting with scenario 1, multiplying the Best £ per pupil by the best-case rolls. We've given cell references from our example in the PDF, but yours may differ if you have a different layout, so please double check everything.

- Firstly, in the 2019/20 column (cell B9 in our PDF example), enter a formula to multiply the 'Best case per-pupil funding' figure in the same column (B6 in our example) by the best-case roll number (B8 in our example).

- Put the cursor on the per-pupil funding reference in your formula bar, then press F4 twice. This will fix the row number (B$6) but not the column number for the £ per pupil reference, which will allow you to copy the first formula to the other years and scenarios in this first set of three. Don't press F4 with the cursor on the rolls reference, as you don't want to fix that.

- Copy and paste the formula in B9 (or drag it) into cells C9 and D9 to populate the fields for 2020/21 and 2021/22 for scenario 1.

- Once you have done that, you can copy and paste the formulae for this row into scenarios 2 and 3 for the middle and worst-case rolls (rows 14 and 19). It will pick up the fixed reference to the Best £ per pupil funding figure and multiply it by the specific roll for that scenario in the line above the formula. Please double check that it has in fact done this.

- Now move on to the second set of three scenarios, which relate to the middle £ per-pupil funding option. In the 'Pupil-led funding total' row for '4. Best case rolls' (cell B27 in our PDF example), enter a formula to multiply the middle £ per-pupil funding figure (cell B24) by the rolls (cell B26). Press the F4 key again to fix the reference to the per-pupil funding value (but don't fix the rolls element) and copy the formula across to the other years in the same row.

- Copy the formulae for all years from this row into scenarios 5 and 6 (rows 32 and 37).

- Repeat the last two steps in the section for the worst £ per-pupil funding option, starting with '7. Best case rolls' Pupil-led funding total in row 45 and copying the formula from that row into scenarios 8 and 9 (rows 50 and 55).

- Double check that all formulae are correct. We have provided a completed example in our PDF document.

******

You should now have a set of nine forecasts across the multi-year period for the pupil-led element of the model. If you change any element of your £ per pupil and roll forecasts, everything should update automatically in the Combinations worksheet. You're well on the way to completing your forecasts for the pre-16 part of your budget.

Adding back excluded items

At the very beginning of our model, we excluded some items from the calculation of funding in activity 2, to achieve an amount per pupil that was mainly driven by pupil data, i.e. pupil-led. To produce a complete set of forecasts for budget share or GAG, we now need to add these items back in.

In most cases, the items that are classified as excluded won't change. It is therefore more a matter of deciding on estimated future values before adding them back into the model. We will talk about the values in a moment.

However, it is very important to identify any 2019/20 items within the MFG exclusions that are one-off in nature. These must **not** be added back in future years. For example, if two schools amalgamate, an additional lump sum is paid in the first year to bring the combined lump sums to 85% of the previous year's allocations across the two schools. This avoids the successor school being immediately disadvantaged by losing one of the two lump sums. The additional lump sum was deducted in item 4 on line 8 in our Best £ per pupil example. Do not add it back in 2020/21 and 2021/22.

The only exception to this rule is if an LA gets approval from the DfE for the additional lump sum to be repeated in a second year, which would normally be no more than 70% of the predecessor schools' lump sums. Then you would need to add back the revised lump sum in the second year, but you mustn't add anything in for the third year.

Another example would be if a school was on split sites in 2019/20 but was later consolidated on a single site. The split site allowance should not be added back from 2020/21 onwards (or whenever the change happened).

Estimating future values for excluded items

In readiness for adding back the excluded items, you need to consider whether the values might change in future years, to make sure your forecasts are realistic.

We created a simple table in our model, to allow a percentage to be inserted which is applied to the previous year's figure for any items that may change. We located this at the end of our Best £ per pupil worksheet, to make it easy to reference the amounts deducted from budget share or GAG. Here's what ours looks like:

	A	B	C	D	E
16	12	Estimated value per pupil (item 9 x item 11)		£ 3,881.54	£ 3,900.94
17					
18			2019/20	2020/21	2021/22
19		Estimated excluded items: future year % change		3%	3%
20	13	Rates LA estimate future years (can be overtyped)	12,460	12,834	13,219
21	14	Other excluded items (3 + 4+ 5) (can be overtyped)	110,000	110,000	110,000
22		Total excluded items to add back	122,460	122,834	123,219

We have separated out rows for items that are likely to change, such as rates, and those that are expected to remain static. The lump sum and sparsity values are only likely to change if your LA is phasing in the NFF.

Rates will vary if you change status at any point after the baseline year, e.g. becoming a Foundation Trust school (LA schools) or converting to academy status. You will be eligible for charitable rate relief which reduces the cost, and your funding will be adjusted accordingly.

Other reasons for changes in rates could be the annual increase in the rate in the pound set by councils, an expansion to meet demographic changes, alterations to your buildings or reviews of rateable values. It can take some time for new rates liabilities to be confirmed, so you may need to contact LA finance officers to find out what's happening.

Academy GAG entered in the £ per pupil worksheets excludes rates. To ensure a complete forecast, you should now add in any rates funding likely to be received. Make sure you are also including the expenditure in your budget plans, to ensure you are comparing like with like.

You might have exceptional circumstances funding to add back, which you will need to estimate. Your LA or the ESFA should be able to advise on any future changes to this.

You can use a percentage change for the above items, applying it only to the items you think will change. Alternatively, you can overtype the individual amounts with the estimates you have decided on. The idea is to create a reference point for the Combinations worksheet.

Activity 14: Adding back excluded items

- Create a table to forecast changes in your excluded items in your Best £ per pupil sheet, using our example if required.
- In the Combinations worksheet, reference the items you are going to add back from the relevant cells for the excluded items in the table. If you are using the same set of values for these items across the years in all of your scenarios, you can use the F4 key to fix the references as we did in the earlier activity and copy the same formulae into all the relevant rows.
- Refer to the PDF section for activities 11 to 14 where we show all the formulae for the Combinations worksheet to check this.
- See our note that follows this activity for guidance if you wish to include best, middle and worst-case options for the excluded items. In a broad-brush approach, it is probably not necessary to do this if the amounts are not particularly significant.

*****

To create different percentage changes across the scenarios for excluded items, you can place separate tables in the best, middle and worst-case sheets. Alternatively, you can enter your estimated values directly.

You have two choices about where to show the variations in these items, depending on whether the changes are likely to respond to changes in the size of your budget or pupil numbers:

- Put the best-case excluded items in scenarios 1, 2 and 3, the middle-case figures in scenarios 4, 5 and 6, and the worst-case figures in scenarios 7, 8 and 9. This follows the £ per pupil element.

- Or: Put the best case excluded items with the best rolls options in scenarios 1, 4 and 7, the middle case figures in scenarios 2, 5 and 8, and the worst-case figures in scenarios 3, 6 and 9. This follows the rolls element.

It's much simpler to keep the same estimates for these items across the different scenarios, so we would avoid varying them, unless you feel they will have a significant impact.

Whichever way you do it, the aim is to achieve a realistic assessment of these costs to add back into the Combinations worksheet. Your totals in the Combinations worksheet should now incorporate these items together with the pupil-led totals.

10 CHOOSING THE FINAL SCENARIOS

Considering the scenarios

You now have nine potential scenarios for the next three years. They all represent different interactions between your predicted per-pupil funding and the number of pupils.

This obviously produces far too many possibilities for you to develop into budget plans, so you need to narrow them down to the final three, representing high-level best, middle and worst-case scenarios. You need to select them in such a way that they decline in value from the best-case to the worst-case.

At this stage, we recommend that you spend some time with your leadership team, to explore which combinations you wish to develop further to the stage of identifying the savings targets you would need to set if they became a reality. It's an important decision, as your future strategic financial planning will hinge on these figures.

But don't forget it is meant to be a broad-brush exercise. If you have created the right expectations, your fellow leaders and governors won't be anticipating total accuracy. The key is in demonstrating the range of possibilities.

Here's a reminder of the matrix of scenarios:

	Best £ per pupil	Middle £ per pupil	Worst £ per pupil
Best roll	1	4	7
Middle roll	2	5	8
Worst roll	3	6	9

Your choices are likely to be affected by your level of confidence in the two elements of the calculations. You might use 1, 5 and 9 if you want to match up the same options for per-pupil values and rolls, but for some schools that will be too simplistic.

Thinking about how likely it is that each of the options could happen and identifying your confidence levels in them will help you to decide which scenarios to run with.

Bear in mind the purpose of this whole exercise: you will be examining the impact of each of the final three scenarios on your budget in order to identify the level of savings needed (or available investment if you're lucky), if your spending plans didn't change. This will lead you to explore what would need to be done to achieve a sustainable budget if any of the three scenarios became a reality.

To guide you in selecting the most appropriate scenarios, consider these examples:

Example 1:

A school has volatile rolls, and its LA is moving towards the NFF, but currently has very high basic entitlement values. The school may be fairly certain that its funding per pupil is likely to reduce but will find it very difficult to predict pupil numbers.

This school is more likely to select from scenarios 7, 8 and 9 than 1, 2 and 3. This approach would reflect the pessimistic forecast for its per-pupil funding, while allowing a variety of pupil number results to be considered.

Example 2:

A popular school with growing pupil numbers whose LA is not adopting the NFF values may believe that their pupil rolls are likely to be in line with the best-case scenario. However, per-pupil funding will be very difficult to project, given that we don't know when the Hard NFF will be implemented.

This school could consider selecting from scenarios 1, 4 and 7 which allow the best-case position for rolls to be included. Through these options the three different possibilities for the unpredictable £ per pupil funding are all being considered. Alternatively, it could select one scenario with either a middle or worst-case roll. There are some things a school can't control, and it's best to be prudent.

There will be a range of options in between these two examples. If you are equally unsure about how per-pupil funding and rolls might develop, you could take any combination of scenarios that provides clear differences, e.g. 1, 5 and 9, or 3, 4 and 8.

Whichever scenarios you choose as your final three, make sure that you place them in order of total funding value from highest to lowest when arranging them in the final scenarios sheet in the next activity. Depending on how significant the percentage changes are for the two elements, the scenario numbering might not produce the total funding values in descending order. Make sure they correspond to a reasonable best, middle and worst-case set of scenarios.

Part of the value of this approach lies in the discussions you will have about which of the scenarios to choose as your final three. The exercise may expose the real level of uncertainty about the two elements involved. Different members of the team might have different views, and it may take some time to reach a consensus.

This will be time well spent, as it will create a common understanding which will underpin future discussions about how to respond to the different levels of funding.

Ideally, your selection will produce three scenarios that have a reasonable distance between them, to make them worth considering. If they are too close together, there won't be much point in spending time looking at alternative solutions to address any shortfall or consider how to spend any extra funding.

Selecting your final three scenarios

Once you have gained agreement from your leadership team to the three scenarios you wish to develop further, make a note of them, taking care to record the reasons why you have chosen them. You will need this later when you are gathering evidence for your Financial Sustainability Plan.

At a later point, you might collectively change your minds about which three scenarios you are going to develop further as full budget plans. There could be a variety of reasons for this; perhaps you've had second thoughts about your assumptions in the initial exercise, or new information might come to light. Having the notes to hand can help you decide whether to explore some of the other scenarios instead, especially if circumstances have changed.

For this reason, we suggest you add a feature to the model which allows you to test out different scenarios before settling on your final three. The easiest way to do this is to put together a lookup table which captures the key figures for the nine options. The best place to build your lookup is at the bottom of the Combinations worksheet, since that is where all of the information resides.

When we reach the stage of designing the Final Scenarios worksheet to incorporate other funding sources as well, this will enable you to simply change a scenario number and all the relevant figures for your budget share/GAG forecasts will automatically be updated. We've found this invaluable as a shortcut when trying to decide which scenarios to choose as the final three.

Activity 15: Creating a lookup for the final scenarios

- At the end of your Combinations worksheet, create a table with a row for each of the nine scenarios, and three sets of columns, each set incorporating the three years of forecasts. Label the sections with the key elements from the Combinations sheet: per pupil funding, rolls and budget share before de-delegation or MAT top slice, as shown below:

1	2	3	4	5	6	7	8	9	10
	Per pupil funding			Roll			Budget share before de-delegation		
	2019/20	2020/21	2021/22	2019/20	2020/21	2021/22	2019/20	2020/21	2021/22
S1									
S2									
S3									
S4									
S5									
S6									
S7									
S8									
S9									

- Number the columns across the top as shown - this enables you to select the relevant information from this table in the Final Scenarios worksheet through a VLOOKUP formula. You will be populating each of the cells by referencing the relevant result from each of the scenarios above the table.
- The initial focus is on the first set of three columns (labelled 2, 3 and 4), where you are going to pick up the per-pupil funding figures for each scenario from the Combinations table, working across the relevant years.
- You can use the F4 key as a shortcut for this section. Start with Scenario 1 (S1). In the first cell under the 2019/20 heading, reference the Best case £ per pupil for 2019/20 (cell B6 in our example), and press F4 twice to fix the row number but not the column number (B$6). Copy and paste (or drag) this cell into the adjoining cells for the next two years to read C$6 and D$6.
- As each of the £ per pupil rows is matched against three roll projections, if you've used the F4 key to fix the row, you can select the Scenario 1 (S1) row of £ per pupil figures for all three years and then copy and paste (or drag) it down into the two rows below for S2 and S3.
- Repeat this process for S4, referencing the Middle case £ per pupil (cell B24) from the Combinations table, and fixing the row number as before. Copy it across the year columns and then copy this set of cells down into S5 and S6.
- Repeat it again for S7, referencing the Worst case £ per pupil (cell B42), fixing the row number and copying it into S8 and S9.
- Move to the second set of three columns (5, 6 and 7) and reference the roll numbers for each of the scenarios, copying them across the years.
- Move to the final set of columns (8, 9 and 10), referencing the total funding for each scenario. Make sure you pick up the **total** line in each case (e.g. B11 for Scenario 1), so that you incorporate both the Pupil-led funding total and the adding back of the MFG exclusions. There's no copying here, because they are all individual amounts.
- Please don't make the mistake of multiplying your per-pupil funding and rolls in the third set of columns in your lookup table. Take the total funding from the relevant cells in the

Combinations worksheet. Otherwise your funding will be understated, because you won't have added back the excluded items.

*****

You've come a long way, and the model is building up nicely. But we want it to be as complete as possible, so there is a little more work to do on some of your other funding sources before you can set up the final three scenarios. It's time to consider what your other funding streams might look like over the next three years.

Our next chapter will consider the various Pupil Premium grants. If these are not particularly significant for your school, you can produce your own estimates manually. But if it is a large element of your funding, you can follow our description of how to use the roll projections you have already prepared as the basis for estimating future Pupil Premium eligibility.

11   PUPIL PREMIUM

Pupil Premium overview

The different categories of Pupil Premium have not been affected by the introduction of the NFF in the initial period from 2018/19 to 2019/20. The individual elements are the same as before: Disadvantage, Service Children, Looked After Children (including those adopted from care and care leavers) and Early Years Pupil Premium.

However, there are some developments which could affect the level of funding you receive from the grant in the next three years, even if there are no structural changes to it. The main areas are the transfer of some funding from the Schools Block of DSG to the Pupil Premium Plus Grant, plus a few issues that could affect eligibility, including Universal Infant FSM and Universal Credit. We will take a look at these before we start to explore the approach to forecasting Pupil Premium funding.

Changes to Pupil Premium Grant Plus

The values in the various elements of Pupil Premium Grant have not changed for some time. There is one exception; the Pupil Premium Plus Grant (PPPG) for Looked After Children (LAC) was increased from £1,900 to £2,300 in 2018/19. But this was not a sign of generosity by the government; it was simply the result of funding being transferred after the LAC factor was removed from the NFF.

During the Soft NFF period up to 2020/21, local authorities can choose to keep a LAC factor in their formula if they wish to do so. Their decision may relate to the historic value of this factor, because most of those LAs that used it provided well above the £400 per eligible child that was transferred in to the PPPG. You can see what each LA decided to do by looking at the file of LA formulae values for 2018/19 which we've already mentioned.

The £400 that the DfE decided to transfer was less than the national average spent in 2017/18. The total allocated to schools was £22.8m; dividing this figure by all the Looked After children across the country produces a calculated average of £645 per LAC.

However, if we take an average for the total spent nationally divided by the LAC numbers in just the 79 LAs that had the factor, the true average is in fact £1,064.

The new approach therefore benefited areas that didn't have the factor in their existing formula and gave insufficient funding to most LAs that had previously used it. There were complaints about this, but the DfE wouldn't change it. However, in discussions about creating a pupil mobility factor during 2018, the Department recognised that extra funding would be needed in order to make allocations to schools which were eligible, but whose LA had not previously applied the factor in the local formula. The mobility factor hasn't been moved into the NFF yet, but at least the principle has been established for future situations like this; however, it is unlikely that the PPPG methodology will be revisited.

In each LA, the Virtual School Head holds the PPPG and can decide how it is spent. Many LAs top slice PPPG to fund the costs of the Virtual School (except for the Head's post, which should be funded from LA resources). There is also an issue that PPPG does not provide any funding for post-16 LAC.

Because of this ability to top slice the grant, schools might not receive the full £2,300 PPPG allocation and LAs could take different decisions about the amount held centrally in future years. If you have pupils who are Looked After in your school, it's worth asking what the LA's proposals are for the rate of grant from 2019/20 onwards.

Issues that affect eligibility

The use of Ever 6 for Pupil Premium provides some protection against volatility in FSM eligibility. Contrast this with the single census point that has been the only FSM measure used by some LAs in the past.

Up to 2017/18, LAs had to choose between this and Ever 6; they couldn't use both indicators.

The NFF now includes both single census and Ever 6 in order to tackle both aspects of deprivation: the cost of providing free school meals (single census) and the wider educational impact of deprivation (Ever 6). From 2018/19 onwards, both can be used in the local formula.

The availability of both indicators could result in a shift in the distribution of deprivation funding within the formula, depending on your local authority's response to the NFF. However, there are other issues at play here which you need to consider when estimating future levels of eligibility for Pupil Premium.

Over the years, shifts in the economy have affected the number of families qualifying for individual benefits that in turn allow eligibility for FSM. This in turn has affected the calculation of Pupil Premium eligibility.

Locally, you may be aware of changes in the jobs market, e.g. large businesses closing or relocating to or from your area. This may inform your predictions of eligibility for new pupils.

In many areas, the introduction of Universal Infant Free School Meals has significantly weakened the incentive for eligible parents to apply until the start of Key Stage 2. As year 6 pupils leave, if fewer Reception and KS1 pupils apply for FSM, this may start to affect the rate of pupils becoming eligible for Pupil Premium grant.

Many schools therefore have to work hard to persuade parents to register. It can be even more challenging for secondary schools, although at least they benefit from several years of eligibility when their students were in primary school.

Schools with pupils who have recently entered the country may find it even more difficult to establish eligibility. There can be significant delays in benefits being confirmed, and we simply don't know how Brexit will affect this.

If you are lucky, you may have an LA that is proactive from a financial inclusion point of view, providing an eligibility checking service that uses data sharing permissions to cross-match information with benefits. We find that most schools recognise the time-saving benefits of buying into such a service; it's a common area of de-delegation of funding decided by LA school representatives on Schools Forums and is frequently taken as a buyback service by academies.

Pupil Premium and Universal Credit

One issue to watch out for in future years in relation to Pupil Premium is the change to Universal Credit. The area in which you are located will play a big part in this; areas involved in the early roll out have seen all children categorised as eligible for FSM as a temporary measure. Universal Credit started in 2013 and is expected to take until 2022 to roll out fully.

Universal Credit is likely to be reviewed regularly as it is rolled out. It is therefore difficult to provide advice on how it is likely to operate at any given time. There are protections for those who were previously eligible for FSM and families who were part of the early arrangements. Because of Universal Infant FSM, these changes in benefits will probably only affect pupils in year 3 and above.

There is a further protection for schools, in that after 2022, eligibility won't be reviewed until a pupil transfers to a new stage of school. Given all these complications, it's probably just as well that schools can check eligibility through the government's database, by going to the Key to Success site (via Secure Access).

The challenge comes when you try to forecast future eligibility. Fortunately, once a child has Ever 6 eligibility, it will continue, so your focus will be mainly on starters and leavers when estimating Pupil Premium funding.

Early Years Premium

The Early Years Pupil Premium (EYPP) was introduced in 2015/16. Three and four-year-olds are eligible if they receive the 15 hours entitlement and their families receive qualifying benefits or if they are a Looked After Child or a care leaver. If a child qualifies for EYPP under several criteria, they will only attract the funding once.

Guidance from the DfE instructs local authorities to fund all eligible early years providers in their area at the national rate of 53p per hour per eligible pupil up to a maximum of 570 hours (£302.10 per year). In cases where a child is also eligible for the additional 15 hours entitlement for working parents, EYPP is paid on the universal 15 hours only, up to a total of 570 hours in the year.

The grant is based on 15 hours per week for 38 weeks. It is the provider's responsibility to identify eligibility. For further information on the categories, please refer to:

https://www.gov.uk/guidance/early-years-pupil-premium-guide-for-local-authorities.

Four-year-olds in primary school reception classes already receiving the school-age pupil premium are not eligible for EYPP funding.

Basis of Pupil Premium Grant projections

Allocations of Pupil Premium Grant are based on January census data rather than the October census (e.g. January 2019 for 2019/20). This is the reason we have to wait so long for allocations; they aren't usually announced until June.

Applying eligibility percentages to your existing roll projections from the October census should suffice for a high-level estimate. The most significant element, the Disadvantage Premium, is fairly stable because of the use of the six-year time span, so one term's data point is unlikely to make much difference.

For service children and Looked After Children, you will probably want to enter your own estimate of the data for each year directly, as the incidence of these children doesn't lend itself to a formulaic approach. You could use a single estimate for best, middle and worst-case options for these elements, since the numbers are likely to be small. Do whatever feels appropriate for your circumstances.

Applying eligibility rates

How you decide to construct your projections of Pupil Premium eligibility depends on whether you have a fairly consistent profile of pupils across all year groups. If you do, you can develop a fairly straightforward worksheet to forecast the changes, based on your total roll projections and your current overall average eligibility rate for the middle case scenario, tweaked for the best and worst-case scenarios.

The Ever 6 approach in the Pupil Premium method is less likely to produce turbulence than the single census count in the main formula. However, if you have a significant difference in eligibility between year groups, especially between leavers and starters, there could be an impact. We have therefore provided a model which uses the roll projections for each year group and allows you to apply variable eligibility rates to them. This forms the basis of Activity 16; our PDF provides an example.

Always consider whether the effort you are putting into an area of your forecasts is worth it - where it will only make a marginal difference to the scenarios, you are better off focusing on other aspects.

You will need to add together the results of Activity 16 with any other elements of Pupil Premium that you are eligible for.

Activity 16: Disadvantage Premium forecasting

- Create a copy of your roll projections worksheet and name it Pupil Premium. You can create an extension at the end of each roll projections option, to forecast the Disadvantage Premium:

	A	B	C	D	E	F	G	H	I	J	K
1			Pupil Premium scenarios - Disadvantage Premium								
2			Primary	Secondary							
3	Disadvantage Premium funding rate		£ 1,320	£ 935							
4											
5	1. Roll projections - best case scenario										
6			R	Y1	Y2	Y3	Y4	Y5	Y6	R-Y6 total	Estimated funding
7											
8	Oct-18	2019/20	44	42	38	44	50	52	51	321	
9	Oct-19	2020/21	48	48	44	39	44	50	52	326	
10	Oct-20	2021/22	48	53	51	45	39	44	50	330	
11											
12	Turnover allowance			10%	5%	3%	0%	0%	0%		
13	Ever 6 eligibility										
14	Eligible pupils	2019/20								-	
15	Eligible pupils	2020/21								-	
16	Eligible pupils	2021/22								-	

- Insert a row above the best-case option and record the Disadvantage Premium rates; these are currently £1,320 for eligible pupils of primary school age and £935 for secondary.
- Working on the best-case option, insert four rows below the turnover allowance row and label them as shown in the example.

- Create totals for the three eligible pupils rows in column J.
- In the Ever 6 eligibility row, enter your estimated eligibility percentages for each year group. You should enter the percentage that relates back to the previous year, in order to reflect the movement of the pupils into the next year group.
- If you wish to show different eligibility rates for 2021/22, you can insert another row for these and apply those rates separately to the final year of the model.
- Enter the actual 2019/20 Ever 6 eligible pupils in row 14.
  In the eligible pupils row for 2020/21, starting with your intake year, enter a formula to reference the roll projection for that year and apply the eligibility percentage. We suggest you use the ROUND function to create whole pupil numbers. For the best-case option, the formula in our example is
  =ROUND(C9*C$13,0), fixing the eligibility rate via the F4 key.
- Copy or drag this formula across to the cells for the remaining year groups, then downwards into the row for 2021/22.
- Create an Estimated Funding heading in column K.
- Create a formula on the row for 2019/22 to multiply the total eligible pupils figure (cell J14) by the relevant Pupil Premium funding rate at the top of the sheet (cell C3 for primary). With the cursor on the funding rate reference, press the F4 key once: (=J14*$C$3).
- Copy this formula down into the rows for 2020/21 and 2021/22.
- When you are satisfied with the formulae, copy these extra four rows and insert the copied cells in the appropriate place in the middle and worst-case options.
- Change the percentage eligibility for years two and three in these other two options if you want to achieve some variations. The 2019/20 eligible pupils are actuals, so they will remain the same.

******

We will now look at the other main funding sources, to help you complete the model.

12   OTHER FUNDING SOURCES

The last stage of the model is to construct a Final Scenarios worksheet which brings together the main budget share or GAG forecasts that you've produced so far with other sources of funding, to produce a full picture of the resources you are likely to receive in the next three years.

Before we show you how to set up the Final Scenarios sheet, we will cover the main sources of other funding. This will help you think about which are most relevant to you and how you want to show them in the model, ready for when you start to build this final worksheet.

It is sometimes challenging to predict what might happen with other sources of funding. Grant regimes may change, and the government can change its mind about the priorities it is prepared to fund, sometimes issuing new grants or ceasing some funding streams.

These other grants will be less significant than your main source of funding, so we're not suggesting you take the comprehensive approach that we used for your budget share or GAG. A reasonable stab at best, middle and worst-case patterns of funding over the three years should be sufficient. As we said in the previous chapter, it's important to ensure that the effort you put in is proportionate to the benefit reaped from a particular activity.

We haven't provided details of how to construct a model for the various areas of funding in this section, because there are so many variations which make it difficult and possibly unhelpful to be prescriptive. Now you've seen how the main forecasting model works, you should have a good idea of the things to consider when deciding on best, middle and worst-case scenarios for each of them. Some will be relevant, and some won't.

Remember to make sure you are only adding grant funding into the final scenarios. Don't include any self-generated income such as lettings, fund-raising from non-government sources, donations or sales income. These are areas of income which broadly relate to discretionary activities, whereas we are trying to build a forecast of government funding that relates to the core function of education. Your budget plan is the place to include income, as part of the net expenditure that will be compared against your funding forecasts.

Nursery funding

For schools with nursery provision, funding can be volatile. The market for early years places in the locality is subject to many influences, and sometimes there is over-provision. There are multiple streams of funding, allocations are provisional until the relevant census data is available, and termly adjustments are made to reflect the actual children taking up the entitlements.

It's therefore easy to understand why it can be challenging to forecast nursery funding even within the current year, let alone for a three-year forecast. But essentially the same elements drive your funding as is the case for the main school budget share: the amount per pupil and the number of pupils. The main difference is that in the case of nursery funding, it's about a termly headcount rather than an annual census.

You can use the same principles to develop your funding forecasts for Early Years as for the main school budget forecasts, but it probably isn't necessary to do three scenarios for each element combined into nine options, as we did for the main budget. Nursery funding is likely to be a relatively small proportion of your overall grants, so we'd advise that you choose just three options: best, middle and worst-case combinations of hourly rates and take up.

Feel free to work out a model that is tailored to your own circumstances; you might use some elements of the main model. We will now present some information for you to consider when deciding what assumptions to make for your best, middle and worst-case scenarios for nursery per pupil funding and roll projections.

Early Years National Funding Formula (NFF)

The Early Years NFF was the first of the new formulae to be introduced, in 2017/18. The component parts of the NFF were used to calculate an overall hourly rate for each LA's 3 and 4-year-olds, as well as for disadvantaged 2-year-olds (although strictly speaking the latter is outside the NFF).

When the 30-hour entitlement for working parents was introduced, it was made clear that the extra 15 hours this represented would be paid at the same rate as the universal entitlement. LAs have to do the same in their local formula.

Transitional arrangements were introduced for the progression of LA funding towards the Early Years NFF, consisting of floor protection and capping of gains. However, in the first year, the maximum loss was much greater (5%), and the cap was much higher (22.9%), than the subsequent Schools NFF. This led to considerable turbulence in allocations to some LAs.

The hourly rates for the 2019/20 Early Years NFF have been announced, and can be found at the following link:

https://www.gov.uk/government/publications/early-years-national-funding-formula-allocations-and-guidance.

For 2019/20, no LA will see a reduction greater than 5% on their 2018/19 overall hourly rate and there is no capping of gains. Only 13 LAs have a lower hourly rate in 2019/20, but the reductions are marginal and mainly affect areas whose original hourly rates were much higher than the average.

The starting position for the Early Years NFF is a universal basic entitlement expressed as an hourly rate, with supplements for additional needs, represented by proxies for Free School Meals, Disability Living Allowance and English as an Additional Language.

The DfE has a policy aim of funding all types of early years providers on a level playing field. LAs have been expected to work towards this, and from 2019/20, they are not allowed to have different hourly rates for different types of providers in local Early Years formulae. The government took this decision in spite of research which showed that primary schools had a higher unit cost than Private, Voluntary and Independent (PVI) settings.

If you have a Maintained Nursery School (MNS) in your local area, it's worth being aware of the issues surrounding the NFF for these settings, as if they are unable to continue, you could be asked to take their children. The research commissioned by the DfE did not even look at MNS costs. They don't have economies of scale to cover their fixed costs of a head teacher with deputising arrangements, the required qualified teacher status and staff:child ratios. The outcry over the imposition of a universal rate led to the DfE providing 'Supplementary Funding' to reduce the impact, but this runs out at the end of 2019/20. Lobbying continues on this matter. At the time of writing, additional funding has been promised but this is a short-term measure.

If the extra funding is withdrawn, many nursery schools may not be able to survive. If you have one nearby, you need to assess the risks involved in being asked to fill the gap in provision, particularly in terms of the impact this might have on your budget. The nursery sector is vocal about the level of funding not covering costs.

Nursery per-pupil funding

As with the Schools NFF, nursery funding only partly depends on government decisions. A local formula operates, which must treat all types of provision in the same way. However, there are no proposals for early years to move to direct funding by the DfE.

There is a cap on central expenditure, meaning the LA can only top slice up to 5% of the Early Years allocation for 3 and 4-year-olds to cover administrative costs and other centrally-held funding. The amount passed on to providers should therefore be fairly stable once your LA reaches the pure formula. This pass-through requirement doesn't apply to funding for disadvantaged 2-year-olds, but we believe that central retention of this element is less common.

The government has specified a list of factors which is more limited than the permitted factors for the Schools Block, so Early Years formulae tend to be simpler. Some LAs use only the two mandatory factors: a basic hourly rate and deprivation, while others also incorporate some or all of the discretionary factors: rurality/sparsity, flexibility, English as an Additional Language and quality (system leadership).

In developing your best, middle and worst-case scenarios for nursery funding per pupil, you will need to consider the significance of each of the factors in your local formula for your school.

Each year, you should be aware of any proposals for change in the Early Years Single Funding Formula in your local area through consultation undertaken by the LA. Schools Forums should discuss any proposals before decisions are made. As we pointed out earlier, anyone can attend Forum meetings as an observer. Minutes and reports must also be available on a public-facing website.

Roll projections for nursery children

Take up of nursery entitlements is one of the more challenging aspects of forecasting your funding. The use of termly headcounts (the method chosen by most LAs) with payments adjusted in arrears can cause volatility.

The best you can do is to look back at trends linked with population changes in your area and make a set of assumptions to use in best, middle and worst-case scenarios. Your LA should prepare sufficiency assessments for early years provision, which can provide some indications of whether there is unmet demand or over-provision in your area. You will also be aware of younger siblings of pupils already attending your school.

In some areas, there are good links between private, voluntary and independent settings (PVIs) and school nurseries. This helps to meet parental needs by facilitating full-day provision. You will then be able to consider the likelihood of places continuing to be filled with a little more confidence. However, in other areas there is high competition between providers and less stability. It all needs to be considered when developing your roll projections for your nursery classes.

The government provides funding for 15 hours for 38 weeks in the universal entitlement. Check if your LA follows this when combining your £ per pupil funding with roll projections to produce your forecasts; some LAs may fund 39 weeks, taking PD days into account.

Other funding for early years

Early Years Premium grant is accounted for within the Early Years DSG rather than the separate Pupil Premium Grant. You can record it under either line in your model, but make sure you only count it once. There is no change to the rate for 2019/20, which is 53p per hour per eligible pupil, up to a maximum of 570 hours (£302.10 per year).

Your LA is required to operate an Inclusion Fund for 3 and 4-year-olds with SEND from the Early Years allocation. There is no requirement to do so for disadvantaged 2-year-olds. Some LAs may already be providing funding from the High Needs Budget for either or both of these groups. The DfE has not specified any values; each LA will decide how to make allocations from the overall Early Years Block and possibly from the High Needs Block as well.

In 2018/1, the government introduced a Disability Access Fund. LAs are required to pass on the allocation of £615 per child in full to settings with children who fulfil the eligibility criteria of receiving Disability Living Allowance and taking up the 15-hour entitlement. It is a lump sum and should not be pro-rated for part-time attendance. Once it reaches the setting, this grant does not have to be spent on the eligible children; it can be used to improve facilities so that the setting can take more children with disabilities in the future. If a child moves part-way through the year, the funding doesn't move with them. The next setting can only claim it from the start of the following financial year.

Inclusion Fund and Disability Access Fund allocations can be included in either the separate line for SEND funding or the Early Years line within the model. We recommend that you make a note of which approach is taken, for future reference.

Don't include any income from extended childcare in your funding forecasts. This is classed as self-generated income and it should be deducted from your gross expenditure when calculating the net expenditure in your budget plan.

Post-16 funding

The post-16 context is rather different from the ever-changing pre-16 situation, because the base rate for full time 16 and 17-year-olds has been frozen (at £4,000) for several years. This funding freeze has also affected the rates for students studying fewer hours. The government has announced that this approach will continue again in 2019/20.

There is a somewhat ironic benefit to this, in that it makes it fairly easy to forecast your per-student funding, especially if you have low levels of additional needs.

The ability to forecast changes in funding therefore relies heavily on the number of students on roll. A key issue will be competition for students. You will already be familiar with travel to learn patterns, the Y11 to Y12 conversion rate from your own school and the intake from other schools in your area.

As well as student numbers, you should consider whether there are likely to be any changes to the programmes offered across the three-year period of your forecasts, as this can affect your future allocations.

Important elements of funding to bear in mind are student retention, higher cost subjects, disadvantage (Index of Multiple Deprivation and low prior attainment blocks) and area costs.

You should ensure you comply with Condition of Funding criteria for students without the relevant Maths and English qualifications, in order to avoid a negative adjustment to your funding. There is a change for 2019/20, whereby students with a grade 2 or below can study towards a pass in functional skills level 2 or a GCSE grade 9 to 4. Once they have achieved this, there is no requirement to undertake further maths or English qualifications to meet the condition of funding. Those with a grade 3 must still study GCSE.

A new post-16 advanced maths premium of £600 per year for students taking a level 3 maths qualification has also been introduced for 2019/20. You can find the details at the following link:

https://www.gov.uk/guidance/16-to-19-funding-advanced-maths-premium.

You can control some aspects of these funding elements, but not all of them. Retention can be improved by better advice when students are choosing their subjects, and by monitoring progress in Y12 to pick up any signs that they are struggling or disengaging. But there can be many external reasons that you can't control.

Formula protection funding to compensate for reductions in allocations will continue until 2020/21, although fewer institutions are eligible for this as the protection tapers.

There are other funding elements to consider, which may or may not apply to your sixth form, such as the Work Placement Capacity and Delivery Fund for vocational level 2 or 3 programmes and the 16 to 19 Bursary Fund.

If you are creating new sixth form provision, you should be aware of the phased calculation for funded numbers when considering the pattern of funding across your three-year period:

- Year 1 - one third of capacity
- Year 2 - double actual recruitment in year 1
- Year 3 - lagged numbers.

The situation may be different for academies funded on estimated numbers with new sixth forms, where funding is agreed with the ESFA.

Use your judgement to decide on the range of possibilities for both your sixth form funding per student and the number likely to be on roll over the three-year period. Because the scope for changes in £ per student is so limited, there is probably no need to go into the level of detail we explored for pre-16 funding; three scenarios for best, middle and worst-case situations should be sufficient.

High Needs funding for post-16 students should be included in the SEN funding section of your forecasting model.

SEN funding

If you've read any of our blogs or listened to the webinars Julie presented in November 2018 for Capita and Schools North East, you'll know that we have serious concerns about the impact of the High Needs NFF. The new formula is not responsive to changes in need, and many LAs are seeing deficits in their High Needs Budgets. Schools are feeling the pressure of providing support for pupils with SEND in the context of inadequate funding in all of the blocks within the Dedicated Schools Grant.

The government has limited the ability of LAs to make transfers from mainstream school budgets to address high needs pressures; no more than 0.5% can be taken from the Schools Block each year with the approval of the Schools Forum, and any request for a higher transfer has to be approved by the Secretary of State.

Decisions on transfers are difficult, because of the state of mainstream school funding. However, moving money from the Schools Block distributes the impact of High Needs pressures more evenly. If LAs have to manage within a ring-fenced High Needs Budget, the savings they will inevitably need to make are likely to penalise schools with specialist provision and those who are inclusive.

This has led to the government requiring all LAs to carry out a review of their High Needs budgets and publish a report on the outcomes. You could see changes to the mix of provision and different thresholds throughout the system, with the consequence that mainstream schools are asked to take and keep more pupils with SEND. Reducing high cost places in the independent sector is likely to be a major focus. Some LAs may also be reviewing the banding systems used to determine top ups.

How can you find out what's happening and how the changes resulting from high needs reviews might affect your school? LAs should have been holding consultation meetings and surveys during their reviews, and the topic will probably have been an agenda item at various network meetings and sub groups. There will have been reports to elected members as well. The Local Offer website for your area is the best starting point; any reports, consultation materials and presentations should be published there. The Schools Forum website is another source of information, since Forum members should be debating any significant changes.

SEND in mainstream classes

Within your budget share or GAG allocation, an element is notionally labelled as being for low-level SEND: the 'notional SEN budget'. This is not an extra allocation. LAs decide that a percentage of certain factors can be deemed to cover low-level SEND, but they can all choose different percentages and indeed different factors. The most common factors selected are low prior attainment, deprivation indicators, and the basic entitlement (on the basis that every classroom teacher will encounter some degree of SEND), but any factor can be included.

You are expected to fund additional support for pupils with SEND costing up to £6k per pupil per year from the notional SEN budget. This is over and above universal provision in mainstream classes, which the DfE assumes costs £4k per pupil, found from overall budget share or GAG. Therefore, you can only claim top up funding for an individual child when you have spent a total of £10,000 between the universal element and the notional SEN budget.

The majority of top ups in mainstream classes will be for pupils with an Education, Health and Care Plan (EHCP), and you should be well aware of these. But some LAs also pay top ups for pupils without plans as part of an early support or inclusion strategy. Bear in mind that this could change as part of the LA's High Needs review.

One other situation where you can claim top ups, which many schools aren't aware of, is where you can prove that you have a higher than average number of pupils with SEND, and that it costs more than your notional SEN budget to support them. It may not be easy to achieve this extra funding allocation, given the pressures LAs are under, but that shouldn't stop you from trying.

Taking all this into account, you should be able to estimate how much you are likely to receive for pupils with SEND in mainstream classes over the next three years. But take care to remove top up estimates at the right time for pupils who are due to leave the school.

SEN units and resource bases

If you have an SEN unit or resource base (LAs use a variety of names for these), bear in mind that the funding system changed in 2018/19. Originally, pupils in the units used to be excluded from the calculation of budget share or GAG, and £10k per place was paid from the High Needs Budget.

Since the change, in theory pupils in the unit/resource base still attract £10k plus top ups, but it is configured differently. You receive budget share for the pupils in the unit, plus £6,000 per pupil and the usual top up. If there are empty places, £10k is paid rather than £6k, because there are no pupils to attract budget share/GAG.

In order to put the money in the right place when this changed, a national transfer of £90m was made from the High Needs Block into the Schools Block, to reflect the extra cost in budget shares.

This means that LAs only have funding in the High Needs Block for the new place-led element of £6k plus the usual top ups, although even that is doubtful, due to the way the High Needs NFF isn't responsive enough to needs.

You'll notice we said 'in theory' when describing the change. The new system assumes that every school receives £4k in budget share or GAG, which isn't always the case. A large primary school in an affluent area with low SEN may receive less than this, and the Minimum Funding Level for primary schools only guarantees £3,500 per pupil. Conversely, small secondary schools and those in areas of disadvantage may receive considerably more per pupil.

A school receiving less than £4k per pupil therefore won't receive the full £10k before it can access top ups, which is detrimental compared to the previous situation. On the other hand, a school attracting £6,000 in budget share will receive place-led funding of another £6,000 before top ups, leading to £12k rather than the old place-led amount of £10k.

To address this unfairness, LAs can adjust top ups to equalise the funding, so that in total, the school receives £10k plus top ups, as before. Not all LAs do this, so it is wise to check. It results in either a positive or negative adjustment on your SEND funding statement.

If you have an SEN unit or resource base, you should be aware of any proposals to change its designation or size. This could be an outcome from your LA's High Needs Review implementation plan.

LAs can negotiate lower top ups for pupils registered in SEN units and resource bases in two situations: firstly, where they want to place a child above capacity, on the basis that fixed costs have already been covered, and secondly where children are placed into empty places, on the basis that the school has effectively received £10k for a place that hasn't been filled for a substantial part of the year. Some LAs have been driven to introduce this approach if it hasn't previously been the practice, because funding is not keeping pace with needs.

Any such moves could significantly affect your funding forecasts, so make sure you have all the facts and can reflect any likely impact in your estimated SEN funding within the model.

Basis of top up calculations

For both specialist provision and mainstream classes, top ups are only paid for pupils actually on roll. The calculation is usually based on the actual number of days, because the funding has to follow the child if they move during the year.

You are advised to examine occupancy trends from the last couple of years, particularly if existing children are approaching a transition point. These will help you decide the levels of top up funding to build into your final scenarios.

Funding for Early Years SEND

In the Early Years section at the start of this chapter, we mentioned Inclusion Fund and Disability Access Fund allocations. These may be quite small amounts but don't forget to add them into the SEN or Early Years funding line, whichever you prefer, in your Final Scenarios worksheet when you reach that stage of the model.

Other grants

The categories of funding to be added into the model under the heading of 'Other grants' will vary, depending on the type of school and the multi-year period under consideration.

We are focusing here on grant funding given by government agencies. As we've already mentioned, any applications to other bodies should be treated as self-generated income and will therefore be offset against expenditure in your budget plan.

Grants come and go, so you will need to keep an eye on the gov.uk website. You can sign up for ESFA bulletins which usually draw attention to changes in grants or rates of funding. Our own free monthly newsletter also picks up announcements. There are other services which provide regular updates; some of these involve paying a subscription, but you might consider it worth the small investment for real-time updates.

One example of a change is the recent announcement of pay grants, for the September 2018 teachers' pay award and the forthcoming increase in the Teachers Pension Scheme employer contribution rate from September 2019. These grants are only guaranteed to March 2020, in line with the end of the current Spending Review period. From 2020/21 onwards, the government could retain them as separate grants or mainstream them into the Dedicated Schools Grant.

For the purposes of your forecasting model, we would suggest placing these in the Other Grants section. At the time of writing, the consultation on the TPS grant has only addressed the question of which types of setting should receive funding, rather than the method for distributing the grant. However, given the pupil-number-driven approach taken to the pay award grant, we would be surprised if the new grant didn't follow a similar methodology. You can therefore use your roll projections with a variety of unit cost estimates for the three scenarios until further information becomes available.

Some of the other grants which you should be aware of, depending on your phase, are:

- Primary PE & Sport Premium
- Primary Music
- Y7 Literacy & Numeracy Catch Up Premium
- Universal Infant Free School Meals

In the past, some academies have received Education Services Grant protection to compensate for significant reductions in the level of grant which occurred when a national rate was established. This is being phased out over several years, so it is unlikely that allocations will continue very far into the three-year forecasting period we are considering, but please check your own situation.

The LA also provides other types of funding. Schools and academies that are expanding to meet population growth at the request of the LA, i.e. to meet basic need for school places, may qualify for support from the local Growth Fund.

From 2019/20 onwards, growth funding will no longer be a historic spend factor but is being brought into the core NFF based on the change in rolls from the previous year (October 2018 compared to October 2017 for 2019/20).

LAs should consult the Schools Forum before deciding the qualifying criteria for growth funding and the method of calculating allocations. Some of it will flow through the formula, where new and growing schools which opened in the last seven years are adding year groups. The LA has to estimate their rolls for the new cohorts from September. If this is relevant to you, please check the arrangement; you may need to go back and adjust your £ per pupil forecasts.

In recent years, some LAs have had a Falling Rolls Fund to support schools which struggle to deliver the curriculum because of declining pupil numbers. This is not intended to support falling rolls caused by parental preference, and it is only available for good and outstanding schools where the places will be needed in the future.

However, the funding previously awarded to LAs for this fund (totalling £8.9m in 2018/19) is no longer available in 2019/20. Instead of separating it out and leaving it as a historic spend factor, or creating a separate factor based on falling rolls, the DfE has absorbed the money into the Growth factor and has paid it out on the growth criteria. This is not mentioned in the documentation for 2019/20; we asked the Department about it directly, and they confirmed this was the case.

This means that if you previously received funding for falling rolls, your LA will no longer be getting any grant for it from the DfE. If you are in this position, we advise you to ask the LA whether they intend to continue the fund or not.

Some LAs have also provided support through a fund for Schools in Financial Difficulty. Published information in Section 251 budget and outturn statements does not specify the amounts separately; they are included in a contingency category, but anecdotally we know that in many areas, this has reduced significantly in recent years.

If you are about to convert to academy status, or have recently converted, you will receive a one-off start-up grant or post-opening grant. MATs may also receive re-brokerage grants for taking on academies from another Trust, and there are a variety of other grants for expansion of the academy system, restructuring costs to address deficits, and to support improvement in performance, whether educational or financial.

Take a prudent approach in predicting the time span for these additional sources of funding - you need to assess the likelihood of them continuing or the rate of grant changing over the course of the forecasting period. In particular, be very careful not to roll forward one-off grants or multi-year grants past their expiry date, otherwise you will overstate your funding and end up with an overspend.

Clawback of funding for exclusions

If you find that your school has a consistent level of exclusions, it would be prudent to make a deduction from your forecasted grants in the Final Scenarios worksheet to reflect the claw back of funding under regulations.

Given the pressures on LA High Needs Budgets, we expect schools to be encouraged to develop earlier intervention and preventative strategies, so you will need to consider what the likely balance will be for your school between the loss of funding via clawback and a change in your expenditure to reflect a different approach to pastoral and other support for vulnerable learners.

If you regularly admit excluded pupils, you could use the same line to record the net position by including any additional funding that you will receive for them. Alternatively, you can create a separate line for this in the worksheet. However, we would advise caution, because the extra funding won't materialise if you don't take the anticipated number of excluded pupils. It's best to avoid over-stating your funding levels.

De-delegation and MAT top slicing

You may need to make another deduction before arriving at an overall total for delegated funding in your final scenarios. There are two situations where this will occur: de-delegation of funding for LA maintained schools, and top slicing of funding by Multi Academy Trusts to pay for services delivered centrally by the trust. If you are a stand-alone converter academy, you won't have either of these elements.

De-delegation for LA maintained schools

Each year, Schools Forum representatives for LA maintained schools are asked to approve de-delegation of specific items. This means that once budget shares have been calculated, an amount is handed back to the LA to run specified services.

The DfE defines the services that can be de-delegated in operational guidance; the actual choices vary from one LA to another, usually as a result of historic decisions. The list for 2019/20 is as follows:

- additional school improvement services
- contingencies (including schools in financial difficulties and deficits of closing schools)
- behaviour support services
- support to underperforming ethnic groups and bilingual learners
- free school meals eligibility checking
- insurance
- museum and library services
- staff costs for supply cover (for example, long-term sickness, maternity, trade union and public duties such as jury service)
- licences and subscriptions, except for those paid for by the DfE and recharged to LAs within the Central School Services Block.

LA maintained school representatives have to take the decision separately for primary and secondary sectors and the result is binding on all mainstream LA maintained schools. For middle schools, costs will be calculated based on the number of primary and secondary aged pupils multiplied by the relevant sector unit costs.

If you are an LA maintained school, now is the time to check that you haven't already deducted de-delegated items from your budget share in the £ per pupil worksheets, otherwise you will be removing them twice.

De-delegation can be calculated using a variety of indicators. We would expect your budget pack to contain a separate statement showing how it has been worked out. The most common method is an overall per-pupil rate, which is easily applied to your roll predictions for the three final scenarios to achieve forecasts for future years. Some items are calculated using specific groups such as FSM pupils, which can be estimated by applying your current eligibility percentage to your roll predictions. For FSM, you should check whether your LA uses single census or Ever 6. EAL is another common mechanism used.

For your worst-case scenario, you could assume that the unit cost will increase by a relatively high rate of inflation each year, and the middle-case could be a modest increase. The best case could be a static unit cost, although that may be unlikely. Each will need to be applied to the relevant roll predictions.

Charge for former Education Services Grant

LAs used to receive Education Services Grant in two parts: Retained Duties grant, covering responsibilities for both schools and academies, and General ESG which related only to functions performed for LA schools (and which was transferred from the LA to academies on conversion).

From April 2017, the Retained Duties element was transferred into local authority DSG allocations and became part of Schools Forum decisions on centrally retained funding (top slicing before the calculation of budget shares). However, the General ESG element was withdrawn from September 2017 for both LAs and academies.

Because the General ESG related to statutory duties which LAs had no choice over, the government allowed them to request de-delegation from their maintained schools. This is an annual decision by LA school representatives on the Schools Forum and is binding on all LA schools for that year. It is a difficult decision, because many of the services, whilst essential, are not particularly visible to schools. However, there would be consequences on other valuable services to schools if this funding was lost, and so many LAs succeed in their requests.

If your LA makes this charge, you should be able to see it on your budget statement. It is usually an amount per pupil; the government has specified that the unit cost should not vary across the sectors.

Please note that we don't know for how long de-delegation will continue. When a Hard NFF is introduced, it seems likely that these services will have to change to a full buy-back arrangement for all types of schools. But as we don't know when this will happen, it's sensible to assume it will continue for the period of your multi-year forecasts.

When it does change, you will have a choice over whether to buy the services or not, but the prudent approach is to continue to deduct it, as it will either be de-delegation, a purchase from your budget or a cost in terms of doing the activities yourself.

MAT deductions from GAG

This section addresses the potential deductions from GAG for individual academies who are part of a Multi-Academy Trust.

If you are a MAT CEO or CFO, you will have a clear understanding of the basis of your Trust's deduction from GAG in order to fund services that are provided by the MAT. It will simply be a matter of making your assumptions for years two and three of the model for each academy's forecasts.

If you are an academy within a MAT and still have local delegated responsibility for your multi-year forecasting, there follows some information to help you with this aspect.

The Academy Trust Survey 2017, which provides some interesting information on this, can be found at the following link:

https://www.gov.uk/government/publications/academy-trust-survey-2017.

The survey report indicated that 75% of the MATs who responded were taking a top slice to provide services. The mean average top slice was 4.61%, with over half of MATs taking between 4% and 5%.

Overall, the survey found that 29% of MATs that responded were varying the top slice, for a range of reasons. The main criteria for the variation were performance (52%), size (38%) and phase (34%). The fact that the percentages add up to more than 100% indicates that combinations of criteria were being used.

You can consider changing the figure for best, middle and worst-case scenarios by making different assumptions about the top slice percentage or about the impact of your roll projections on a top slice per-pupil, depending on the methods used.

Pooling of GAG at MAT level is also increasingly under consideration. This may be due to the turbulence caused by the NFF, particularly in MATs which cross LA boundaries. It may also be driven by funding pressures which affect different types of academy in different ways.

The survey referred to above stated that 18% of 267 respondents were currently redistributing GAG within the trust, and 31% intended to do so in the future. However, the recent Kreston Academies Report produced different results, indicating a lower level of interest in pooling of GAG.

We said earlier that we advise MATs to undertake forecasting individually for the academies within the trust and then amalgamate the results to see the overall possibilities for future funding. This exercise could prompt a re-evaluation of the level of top slicing of GAG, as you see the projections and consider whether further centralisation could achieve efficiencies to improve financial sustainability across the MAT.

Purchase of LA services by academies

As an academy, you won't see de-delegation on your GAG statement because it's specific to LA maintained schools. However, you usually have the choice of buying the equivalent services from the LA. This will not be a deduction from GAG but a cost from your budget. This isn't relevant to the model; it's just a reminder to incorporate it when you get to the stage of your budget forecasts.

If you haven't read the section in this chapter on LA de-delegated services, go back to take a look at the list and consult your local Schools Forum's budget reports to see what is on offer for buyback. Services such as free school meal eligibility checking are often relatively low in cost compared to the work involved in doing it yourself.

13 PREPARING FINAL SCENARIOS

Constructing three final scenarios

You've persevered through all the stages of building your scenarios and considering the different funding streams that you need to include. Congratulations! Now you can bring everything together in a set of three final scenarios.

Activity 17: Setting up the Final Scenarios worksheet

- Create a new worksheet labelled Final Scenarios.
- Set up a table as shown in the following example.

	A	B	C	D	E	F
1			Final Scenarios			
2						
3			Scenario reference	2019/20	2020/21	2021/22
4		**Best case**				
5	1	Per pupil funding				
6	2	Roll				
7					£	£
8	3	Budget share/GAG (before de-delegation/top slice)				
9	4	Pupil Premium				
10	5	Nursery funding				
11	6	Post 16 funding				
12	7	SEN funding				
13	8	Other grants				
14	9	Exclusions claw back/funding for admitted pupils				
15	10	Less de-delegation/MAT top slice				
16				-	-	-
17		Change year on year			-	-
18		Cumulative change			-	-

- We shaded our cells to make sure that items needing input (the scenario reference at the top and items 4 to 10 for the non-core funding streams and deductions) can be distinguished from the items that will be referenced from your look up table in the Combinations worksheet. You can see it in colour in our PDF.
- Copy this section and paste it twice in the same worksheet. Then change the titles of the copied sections to show middle and worst-case scenarios.

******

Starting to populate the Final Scenarios worksheet

Now we need to create formulae to populate the per pupil funding, rolls and total budget share or GAG before de-delegation or top slice, using the lookup table you created in Activity 15.

If you haven't used the VLOOKUP function before, or need a reminder of it, the essence is that it searches a defined range of cells to find a match with a particular name or reference, and then delivers the value from a specified cell within that range. The cells in the lookup table that you are seeking a match with must be in alpha or numerical order; ours are, from S1 to S9.

We are going to search the lookup table from Activity 15 for the scenario number you've chosen, starting with the best-case scenario then enter a formula to deliver the relevant values for the £ per pupil, roll and total funding before de-delegation and top slice for each of the years. We will add in the other sources of funding as the last step.

Our PDF example shows you the function arguments box for the VLOOKUP function which we have used in our own worksheet. There are three parts to the function:

- Lookup value: in this case, this is the scenario reference in the Final Scenarios worksheet, e.g. S1, that you want to tell Excel to find in the lookup table within the Combinations sheet;
- Table array: the full range of cells in the lookup table that you want Excel to search in, to find the values to populate the relevant Final Scenarios cells;

- Column index number: the number you've recorded at the top of the column that you want to take the data from.

Activity 18 shows you how to complete this function.

Activity 18: Populating scenarios from the lookup table

- Type in S1 in the best-case cell in column C. Don't worry if you haven't chosen that as one of your final scenarios. At this stage it is simply to give you a point of reference as you test out the formulae. You can change it later and see the figures being automatically updated.
- Create a VLOOKUP formula to pull across figures from the table. If you are familiar with this function, you can go ahead without our help. If not, read on.
- With the cursor on cell D5, click on 'fx' which you will find to the left of the formula bar. Type in VLOOKUP, then double click on it within the list to bring up the function arguments box.
- Click in the lookup value field, then click on the scenario reference (S1 in our example) in the Final Scenarios sheet (cell C4) and press F4 to fix both the column and row reference.
- Now click in the Table Array field in the function arguments box and then click over to the Combinations worksheet. Select the lookup table, making sure you click on the S1 label in the first row below the column headings, then hold down the mouse button and move to the very last cell in the line for S9 (the column you've numbered as 10). Release the mouse then press F4 to fix the full range of cell references ($A$69:$J$77).
- Click into the Column index number field in the function arguments box and manually enter the column number for the item you want to appear. In the case of the 2019/20 best case per pupil funding, this will be column number 2.
- Select ok; you should see the best-case per pupil funding figure for 2019/20 appear in cell D5.

- Now, because you've fixed the references to the scenario number and the table array, you can copy and paste (or drag) this formula across the row for the best-case per pupil funding cells for 2020/21 and 2021/22. The initial result will be the same figure, because it's still referencing column 2.
- You now need to edit the formula to change the column index number at the end of the formula to 3 for 2020/21 and 4 for 2021/22. Check the results against the Combinations worksheet to make sure you are picking up the correct figures.
- It's easy to populate the next elements; all you need to do is copy the formula from the first row into the rolls and budget share/GAG rows. Then go into each cell and amend the column index number at the end of the formula. To pick up the roll forecasts from the lookup table, this should be columns 5 to 7 going across the row, and to pick up budget share/GAG it will be columns 8 to 10.
- Check the figures against the Combinations sheet to make sure they are correct. Now change S1 to your chosen best-case scenario if yours is different, and make sure that the figures change to the correct values.
- You can now copy the formulae for these rows from the best-case scenario into your middle and best-case scenarios. The only amendment you need to do is to change the reference to the correct scenario number field, otherwise it will still produce the figures for the best-case scenario.
- At the bottom of each of our scenario tables, we've put a calculation to track the change between years and a cumulative effect to show the scale of the change from the baseline. You don't have to do this if you don't want to, but we find it quite effective when comparing the three scenarios.
- Refer to our PDF if you want to see how we did this activity and double check the formulae references.

******

Adding in other funding streams

Now all you need to do is transfer forecasts for your other sources of funding into the Final Scenarios sheet. If you have constructed your own worksheets within the model for some of the items, you can create formulae to pick up the figures from there. Otherwise, it will be a matter of keying in your forecasts.

If you have created a Disadvantage Premium worksheet within the model, you can reference the relevant cells in the estimated funding column. But if you have any eligibility for the other elements of Pupil Premium, you will need to add these into the formula.

Make sure that the totals in the Final Scenarios worksheet pick up the correct rows to achieve accurate forecasts of total funding across the three-year period for each of the three scenarios.

You will probably want to return to this section of your funding forecasts on a regular basis, as further information becomes available on the government's intentions following the Spending Review. At the time of writing, we haven't seen any indications of the timeline for this, but it seems unlikely that any detailed information will be available by the time academies have to submit their three-year budget forecast at the end of July. LA schools usually submit their budgets to the local authority during the summer term.

Sense checking

We encourage you to scan the results in your Final Scenarios worksheet to make sure that they appear sensible. Have you included the correct rows in your totals? Do the scenarios go from a higher figure down to a lower figure? If not, consider swapping round some scenario numbers.

Remember the purpose of the exercise, which is to achieve a meaningful difference in funding levels between the three options. If this isn't possible, review your assumptions. If there really is a lot of stability for your school, you could decide to work with only two options. But we anticipate that this would be rare, given all the uncertainties about the various aspects of the school funding system.

Do your other sources of funding look reasonable? Have you been over-optimistic, or do your assumptions stand up to challenge? Make sure they are robust; testing them out in discussions with governors can be a really useful exercise.

Make careful notes of the assumptions that you have used in choosing the final scenarios. In some cases, particularly the other funding streams, there will be a direct link to your expenditure plans. If you have made assumptions on ring-fenced funding in your forecasts, you will need to allow for expenditure on those functions within your multi-year budget. This is particularly important for SEN funding, but you should carefully check the conditions of all grants to identify where this could be an issue.

Reviewing the scenarios

You will be very pleased to have completed the tasks, having reached the stage when you can put the results into your budget planning software to identify what issues arise in relation to your current spending plans. Your normal approach to budget setting takes over at this point, but it will be far better informed because you have three scenarios to consider.

It's tempting to complete the process and forget about your forecasts. You'll want to focus on deciding how to respond to any gap that emerges between the funding in each scenario and your spending plans.

But circumstances change, and it is advisable to make a note in your diary to carry out a termly review of the assumptions. The model makes it easy to change individual elements of your forecasts, such as the percentage change in your funding, your admissions intake estimates and pupil turnover allowances.

If your formulae are operating as intended, everything should update automatically, producing new versions of your scenarios. From time to time you should check whether your final three scenarios are still the right ones. Don't forget to keep the other funding streams under review as well.

Outcomes of the future funding model

Congratulations on having persevered with all the activities and on producing nine options, which you have whittled down to the final three scenarios. You will have done a lot of thinking about the assumptions that underpin the model; we are sure this will have produced some significant debates. It will also have enhanced the understanding of your fellow leaders and governors about how things may change in relation to your school's financial position in the future.

As we discussed in one of our earliest chapters, all of this preparatory work will have highlighted the levels of uncertainty you are dealing with. It will hopefully have relieved some of the pressure from your colleagues to provide accurate figures. The situation is far from clear cut, and our methodology helps to emphasise that fact.

Throughout this process, you will have involved your senior leaders and governors, and potentially other staff, in the development of your assumptions. By debating them and risk assessing them to ensure that they stand up to challenge, you will be well equipped to use the scenarios as the basis for your multi-year budget plan, which combines your funding forecast and expenditure forecast for the next three years.

The level of detail in the model should give assurance to your funding body that you have taken the responsibility of multi-year financial planning seriously. You have focused on the strategic issues while paying attention to detail, using all the intelligence, both hard data and soft information, to good effect. This sort of exercise can only enhance your standing as a leader within your school, academy or MAT.

You now need to convey the results of your work to staff, governors and other interested parties. Our favoured method for doing this involves developing a Financial Sustainability Plan, which sets out the process you have gone through and the conclusions you have reached.

You may have your own version of this, but if not, our next chapter will outline an approach and a suggested template for you to get the message across.

14 YOUR FINANCIAL SUSTAINABILITY PLAN

You now need to set out your path to financial sustainability in a way that explains the results of your forecasting activities and multi-year planning to your funding body, staff, governors and other interested parties. This chapter will explain how you can confidently produce a Financial Sustainability Plan (FSP), using all the information and calculations that you have already developed.

Purpose of a Financial Sustainability Plan

The purpose of a Financial Sustainability Plan (FSP) is to draw together the process you have followed in forecasting your school's funding, show how you have produced your multi-year budget projections and explain the conclusions you have reached. An action plan will be presented outlining how solutions can be implemented to resolve any anticipated shortfall, or how additional resources can be used wisely to support school improvement.

It will be a succinct, coherent and presentable document which can be used to explain your financial strategy to a variety of interested parties such as governors, senior leaders, your funding body and Ofsted or other relevant inspectorates.

The FSP should be a working document which is updated on a regular basis, at least annually, or more often if you know there has been significant change.

The need to update it might come about from a change in pupil numbers since your initial estimations, or an announcement from the government in relation to school funding. On the other hand, it may be that you have new information relating to expenditure which will significantly affect your multi-year budget plans. You need to judge if the changes you are making are material enough to warrant an update during the year.

Whether updated mid-year or not, this working document should be used continuously throughout the year. The purpose of the FSP as far as senior leaders are concerned is to inform strategic decision making. It should be referred to whenever you are taking decisions on staffing, reviewing the curriculum or producing your school development plan for the year ahead.

Linking all your plans is essential for the achievement of value for money education. Integrated Curriculum-Led Financial Planning is a key technique currently being promoted to assist with this. Your FSP helps to bring together all aspects of the school's planning processes, linked to your overall vision.

For governors, the FSP provides an important insight into the school's medium-term planning, giving a solid evidence base and assurance that backs up the decisions you are asking them to take throughout the year. For funding bodies and Ofsted, the FSP gives a reassurance that the school is a going concern and that performance can be sustained into the future.

Benefits of the FSP

A Financial Sustainability Plan gives you an opportunity to present your medium-term financial plans to your staff, governors and funding bodies with a greater degree of confidence about the level of funding you may receive in the future. It sets out clearly the direction you are leading the school in, explains the assumptions you have made in reaching your conclusions, and allows you to share the evidence on which they are based.

The FSP is relatively easy to compile, because you have already completed most of the work by following the process in this book. The notes you have made throughout will be invaluable in speeding up the process. Your plan provides a structure for collating everything you have done so far into one professional and coherent document.

It can also be quickly and easily updated each time your funding forecasts and/or multi-year budget projections are updated, to give context to the plans as they change.

Structure of the plan

<u>The basics</u>

It is important to make your FSP look professional. Simple things will make a big difference, such as a title page with your school logo, the name of the document (Financial Sustainability Plan), the years it covers and the date of preparation (amended for future updates). Do you have a house style for your school improvement planning documents? If you adopt this style, you are emphasising that the FSP is an integral part of a suite of planning documents that collectively drive the school forward.

Ensure you use clear page numbering, as you may need to jump around the FSP in your presentation of it and you want your audience to easily be able to keep up with you. Include a contents page with links to each of the sections. It may sound simple, and it is, but without this you run the risk of the reader becoming lost and not understanding the structure of the plan.

MATs may need to consider whether to produce separate plans for each academy or show the overall plan in a single report.

<u>The content</u>

While you are free to decide your own structure, these are the main sections we would expect to see in a Financial Sustainability Plan:

1) Introduction
2) Approach to multi-year funding projections
3) Best, middle and worst-case scenarios for future funding
4) Comparison of future funding with current expenditure plans
5) Multi-year Budget Plan
6) Action Plan
7) Appendices

<u>The detail</u>

1) Introduction

You may choose to write your own introduction, explaining what an FSP is and what the purpose of it is in the context of your school. We have provided a sample introduction in Appendix 1, which you may use if you wish. This is generic enough to be used for any school.

Importantly, it sets the scene for the reader to gain an understanding of what the FSP is trying to achieve.

2) Approach to multi-year funding projections

The purpose of this section is to explain how you have constructed the forecasts of your funding to facilitate the production of the multi-year budget projections. Here you need to describe the process you have been through in following the activities and be very clear about the assumptions that underpin them.

You should provide a rationale for your key choices in the various stages of the model, accompanied by clear evidence. Show how you have consulted colleagues and specialists in order to obtain relevant information and how you have applied it to the key elements within the model.

Soon you will see how important it is to include the results of the activities you have undertaken as appendices to your FSP, in order to provide an evidence base for your assumptions and conclusions. This is the section where you will describe what you did and reference those appendices.

You may experience challenge and debate when presenting your FSP; this should be welcomed as part of the ongoing process. It will allow you to review and refine your funding projections where necessary.

Because this section will be strongly tailored to the context of your own school and the assumptions you have made, we can't provide a generic example of how you might display your workings for the different options and combinations in your appendices.

However, you can use our approach of taking screenshots (we used the Windows Snipping Tool) and saving them as images, as we've done for our accompanying PDF document.

3) Best, middle and worst-case scenarios for future funding

Here you will include the summary of final scenarios across the three years to show the outcome of your modelling. You could show the full nine options in an appendix, if you want to emphasise the range of possibilities.

You will provide notes that draw attention to particular issues or features, explaining the reasons for your final choices. This section will move the reader from the general principles and assumptions described in the previous section to specific aspects of the final scenarios you have chosen.

It's advisable to make it clear that these scenarios can be amended as further information becomes available. You could indicate the sort of circumstances that might make this necessary or desirable.

This section can conclude with a clear statement of the best, middle and worst-case funding forecasts.

4) Comparison of future funding with current expenditure plans

This section is very important and will be specific to your school's circumstances. It will show what happened when you compared your future funding with the school's current expenditure plans. Crucially, it will highlight any significant gaps between the resources that you expect to receive over the multi-year period and what you currently plan to spend.

The content of this section naturally depends on the outcome that you experience, i.e. a shortfall, a match or a surplus. You need to quantify the extent of any savings needed or any surplus funding that might be available under each of the scenarios.

An accompanying commentary will be needed, to explain what each scenario is showing and what this means for your school; this is an essential part of the FSP. It will reassure your audience of the depth of your understanding, aid their own comprehension and add deeper meaning to the plans.

You may also want to include here any details of assumptions you have made in your current expenditure plans, as these will eventually influence or limit the solutions in the next section of your plan. For example, how have you estimated the September 2018 cost of living rise for teachers' salaries across the period, and what was the outcome of the associated pay grant awarded so far for 2018/19 (part year) and 2019/20 (full year effect)?

We recommend that you describe here any provision for other known cost pressures, such as the increase in employer pension contributions for the Teachers Pension Scheme from September 2019. You will need to make some assumptions about what the government means by the statement that this will be fully funded. There could be a risk of winners and losers as there was for the teachers' pay award. Issues like this need to be kept under review to identify any new information as it is published.

As with the funding forecasts, be prepared for challenges and have your evidence ready for a detailed discussion. Achieving consensus will be vital in order to make the next stages of the process work.

These matters can be presented in any format that you feel appropriate for your school and the way you work. They could be taken directly from financial forecasting software reports or you may choose to produce your own using spreadsheets.

The aim of this section is to set the baseline position, i.e. showing what would happen if your funding forecasts came to fruition and you had not acted but had maintained expenditure at the current planned levels.

This sets the scene for the next section, where you identify strategies to make good any shortfall or allocate any surplus wisely to support your school improvement strategy.

5) Multi-year Budget Plan

This part of the FSP represents your response to the funding changes. In this section, you need to present your suggested solutions for any forecasted reduction or increase in funding and show the new version of your multi-year budget for each of the three final scenarios. While the best and worst-case scenarios are less likely than the middle-case, you need to agree how you would respond if they did become a reality.

If your school is facing funding challenges, leaders and governors will need to agree what the solutions might look like. Alternatively, if additional funding is a likely scenario for you, how might you deploy this funding? Have you quantified the cost pressures that need to be covered first?

Remember that these projections are only estimates. It is important to be prepared; you may be hopeful that your funding will increase, but until that becomes a reality, you should not spend in anticipation of what is not yet realised.

Similarly, be careful that your potential solutions are not overly pessimistic. At present they are only a possibility. In some cases, you may need to start implementing them early, but in others you simply need to know what your solutions will be, should you need them.

We advise creating a timeline plan setting out the solutions for each of your three final scenarios. You may need to prove to your funding body that a time-limited recovery plan is feasible if there is any risk of the school falling into deficit.

Whilst staffing is likely to be the main area of consideration for any required savings, there may be other areas of the budget which can become more efficient.

Apart from staffing, are there any areas of budget expenditure that could be easily reduced with little or no impact on the quality of education your school provides? Even if some negative impact is unavoidable, is this preferable to reducing staffing levels? Can income generation be pursued more vigorously?

When asking yourself these questions, remember always to consider the principles of value for money. Pay particular attention to the impact that you expect to see from existing or reduced spending in each area. For detailed advice and guidance, see our book, 'Leading a School Budget Review'. It deals with the cultural issues as well as the practical processes for examining all the areas within your budget.

Your school's response to potential funding changes is probably the most difficult part of the process you have embarked on. We advise using the FSP to involve the rest of your senior leadership team in developing solutions. This is a strategic school improvement planning process, not just a budget exercise. The overarching view of all senior leaders is critical to securing the appropriate response to support your school's continuous improvement.

6) Action Plan

Your action plan will be tailored to your school, detailing the next steps you need to take in order to achieve a sustainable budget. This is the culmination of all your work so far, using the information you have prepared and the proposed solutions to identify specific actions, which will be taken by named individuals.

The action plan should clearly show the responsibilities of individuals and teams, as well as some indication of the timelines for all of the key actions required to achieve the necessary changes in your budget.

The actions should be specific, organised within broader headings such as staffing restructures, re-negotiation of contracts and income generation strategies.

Be clear about the expected outcomes from each action and show how, by whom, and at what intervals progress and completion of the action plan will be monitored. Knowing how you will take corrective action if the plan is not on target is important.

Don't forget to identify any resources that will be needed to make the action plan happen. Some solutions may require a small investment in order to secure savings. You must be able to identify the impact in each financial year, as the basis for your three-year budget.

7) Appendices

Your appendices should contain the outputs from the activities you have worked on throughout the book. These will build a sound evidence base for the information you are presenting in the main body of the plan and we strongly recommend that you include them.

Here is a checklist of the worksheets you will complete in the process, to guide you in your list of appendices:

- Best, Middle and Worst £ per pupil worksheets;
- Roll projections worksheet;
- Combinations of per pupil funding and roll projections;
- Disadvantage Premium forecasts (if used);
- Your own worksheets for nursery, post-16 and other Pupil Premium funding, plus any other funding sources as applicable;
- Final scenarios bringing everything together.

For the sections relating to your multi-year budget plan, you will have an existing format for your budget reports. Consider whether this is fit for purpose in the light of what your FSP shows; could it be presented more clearly? Is it meaningful and clear to the reader?

Updating and refining the plan

Your multi-year budget projections should be updated at least annually, but it may be necessary to amend them mid-year if new information becomes known that would make a material difference and affect your overall financial management strategy.

We recommend that you develop an audit trail of any changes made and the justification for them. There could be problems at a later date and you or other leaders may need to identify the reasons why a different approach was taken.

When you make an update to your multi-year budget projections, the following parts of the FSP may need to be updated to reflect the change:

1) Introduction: an explanation of why the update is needed.

2) Approach to multi-year funding projections: any changes to the assumptions you have made.

3) Best, middle and worst-case scenarios: replace any that have changed, including the selection of different options for the final three.

4) Comparison of future funding with current expenditure plans: re-calculate the differences if the changes significantly alter your school's overall position, from a surplus to a deficit or vice versa, or if there is a change in the projected level of funding.

5) Multi-year budget plan: review your interpretation of any significant changes to projections to accommodate any movement in your financial position.

6) Action plan: update actions in accordance with any significant changes in the overall picture for your school and check whether the timeline is still realistic.

7) Appendices: update the relevant worksheets in your appendices if any of the changes relate to your funding forecasts or expenditure plans.

Using the FSP for financial leadership

We have talked about the concept of financial leadership in our previous books and in our blog posts. Essentially, financial leadership is about all leaders having ownership of and shared responsibility for the school's finances in the most strategic sense.

This means having an awareness of the school's financial position, understanding how the school's financial plans link to all other school improvement plans and getting the financial culture in the school right, by role-modelling desired financial behaviours amongst all stakeholders.

The FSP is a key element in achieving strong financial leadership in your school. It helps to make some of the complex issues and challenges your school is faced with more understandable and it provides a real insight into what lies ahead.

Involving senior leaders and governors throughout the process of forecasting your school's budget, particularly when estimating your future pupil numbers, encourages challenge and debate, deepening their awareness and understanding.

For schools whose financial position is challenging, the FSP may trigger a fundamental budget review, the process for which we explain in detail in our book 'Leading a School Budget Review'. It is essential that staff are engaged in the process of a school budget review to secure its long-term success. The FSP provides solid evidence to persuade interested parties that a school budget review is needed and gets buy-in from staff from an early stage.

You will be conscious of the need to report the information you have to the Governing Body. There are a number of reasons for this, but primarily the Governing Body holds school leaders to account for pupil outcomes, overall school improvement and achieving a balanced budget. The FSP is an effective way of presenting the information.

Remember that you will also need the Governing Body's approval to enter into a consultation with staff for a staffing reduction, if this is needed. The earlier the Governing Body are aware that this is a possibility, the more understanding and supportive of this proposal they should be.

The FSP can also be a useful tool in discussions with unions in a restructuring situation, as you will be able to prove that your proposals have emerged from a thorough consideration of the options.

Presenting the FSP

Always provide your audience with the FSP prior to the meeting in which you present it. For governors, this should be ideally be seven days before the meeting. They will need time to digest the information, to enable them to make any meaningful challenge and to contribute to the debate during the meeting.

You may be worried that the information could be difficult to understand and even intimidating for some, without the context that you would provide in your face-to-face presentation. Assure colleagues or governors that you will present the information in full at the meeting and will answer any queries or questions they may have to give the appropriate background information.

If you follow our guidance to develop your FSP, it should be clear enough for most people to get to grips with. You may be concerned about the content itself; for example, one of your multi-year budget projection scenarios may indicate a future potential deficit. It is still wise to give your audience time prior to the meeting to understand the document, but when you send it out you may want to point out in your accompanying correspondence that the detail of the figures needs to be understood within the context of the full explanation that you will provide at the meeting.

When presenting the plan to governors, senior leaders or any other audience, it is important to get the balance right between pessimism and optimism. If you are overly pessimistic in your approach, you may influence colleagues to react with a cost cutting strategy which may involve staff redundancies that don't turn out to be necessary.

If you are overly optimistic, the opposite may happen, which could be just as catastrophic. If the need for a staffing review is ignored in the hope that the school won't actually end up in that position, the school could find itself facing a deficit position without sufficient time to restructure and make the necessary savings. This could result in more punitive cuts than an earlier and more measured approach.

A health warning is needed when presenting your information, to explain that a broad-brush approach has been used and that the forecasts are subject to a number of variables which could change. The emphasis should be on planning ahead at an early stage, in order to buy school leaders time to think strategically and sensibly about their response.

The FSP can help you to plan ahead in order to prevent a potential deficit position in the future, or it may guide you in considering how you would use additional resources. Either way, you should think carefully before implementing either strategy and ensure that you are confident in the component parts of your forecasting. You can allow for a margin of error and tailor the action plan as you become aware of any changes in your funding forecasts.

Having a plan will make you better prepared for any unexpected events, because you will know the direction of travel to follow and will not have to take decisions from scratch. You can re-read our chapter on scenario planning as a reminder of all the benefits.

15 CONCLUSIONS

Summary of the process

We hope you have found our approach to forecasting your future funding to be helpful. It is the one thing that many schools have not attempted, due to the lack of firm information, yet it can make a significant difference to the robustness of budget projections.

Having gone through this process, you will have a much better understanding of the most important influences on your future funding. You have given careful thought to the possibilities and the risks they might pose, and you have challenged yourself to make sure your assumptions are robust.

In following the recommendations we've made, you are taking an important and proactive set of steps towards financial sustainability. As further information becomes available, it will be easy for you to return to the model and update the scenarios. It is an approach which can raise your profile as a responsible, thoughtful and intelligent leader.

We welcome feedback, so please get in touch with any thoughts you have on the process, especially if you can think of any ways of improving the model, or if you have found it particularly valuable in securing agreement from senior leaders and governors to take action to prevent a deficit.

We would be particularly grateful if you could spare a few moments to leave a review on the page where you purchased the book. This not only guides us in whether we are succeeding in our aim to provide useful tools, but it also helps to make our books visible to others, so we can help more people in the education community.

16   KEEP IN TOUCH

Everything we do at School Financial Success is designed to provide advice and support for different aspects of school financial leadership. We write regular blog posts at our website (see below for the web address) and produce a free monthly newsletter with news of government announcements, consultations and media stories on key issues from the world of school funding and finance. Subscribers to the newsletter receive a detailed analysis of any important announcements on school funding reform.

The first two School Financial Success guides have a focus on budgeting: 'School Budget Mastery', which provides an overview of how to prepare a budget and monitor progress against it, and 'Leading a School Budget Review', which outlines change management techniques for those tasked with leading a review and provides prompts for reviewing specific areas of the budget. There are links to the sales pages for the books on our website.

Our website will be kept updated with news of topics we are planning to write about, and we welcome suggestions for future subjects that you would like us to tackle in subsequent books.

There are a number of ways you can keep up to date with our latest news about school funding, depending on your preferred type of media:

- our website at https://schoolfinancialsuccess.com
- a public Facebook page for School Financial Success at http://bit.ly/20REuM8
- our Twitter feed 'JulieCordiner_School Financial Success' at @juliecordiner.
- LinkedIn - our separate accounts:

https://www.linkedin.com/in/juliecordiner/ and
https://www.linkedin.com/in/nikola-flint-704880136/

We'd love to see you at any of the above places. There is a contact form on our website if you want to get in touch directly, via schoolfinancialsuccess@outlook.com.

Thank you for reading Forecasting Your School's Funding. We wish you every success in your journey to a sustainable budget.

Julie Cordiner & Nikola Flint

Appendix 1

Sample introduction for FSP:

Uncertainties in future funding for schools, particularly with the introduction of the National Funding Formula (NFF), and the increasing cost pressures schools are facing, mean that early financial planning for the future is critical to a school's financial success.

The purpose of this Financial Sustainability Plan is to ensure and prove continued value for money education for '(ENTER SCHOOL NAME)'. This can involve the following, depending on local circumstances in any given period:

- awareness of future funding possibilities;
- a high-level plan to respond to changes in funding;
- the efficient and effective use of available resources;
- prompt action to avoid a deficit budget, or if unavoidable, preparation of a deficit recovery plan.

The Financial Sustainability Plan details a variety of strategic assumptions about future funding, which is the missing piece of the financial planning jigsaw. It culminates in a series of multi-year budget projections for '(ENTER SCHOOL NAME)'.

These budget projections are based on scenario planning techniques which produce best, middle and worst-case scenarios for funding forecasts. These are used as the foundation of a series of multi-year budget projections. The Financial Sustainability Plan is designed to inform future financial planning and decision making for school leaders and governors.

The background work that has been carried out by school leaders to inform this plan is thorough and detailed. All activities undertaken can be found in appendices to this report. The main body of the plan focuses on the multi-year budget projections, interpretation of these different funding scenarios, response to funding changes and an action plan for financial leaders.

ABOUT THE AUTHORS

Julie Cordiner

Education Funding Specialist

I'm a qualified accountant and independent consultant specialising in school funding and education finance, with over 35 years experience in local authority education work, including 10 years as an Assistant Director. Between 2007 and 2015 I was a member of the DfE's advisory group on school funding. I advise schools and local authorities on school funding and achieving value for money in order to support better outcomes and enable children and young people to maximise their potential, something I'm passionate about. Everyone deserves the best possible education and we all need to use taxpayers' money wisely, to achieve a fair chance for every single pupil.

Nikola Flint

Chief Financial Officer

With a background in accountancy and sixteen years experience in the school business management profession, I fulfil a broad, strategic role as Chief Financial Officer in a multi-academy trust, leading on all aspects of school organisation and SMSC. My experience as a Specialist Leader of Education offering school-to-school support has widened my perspective of the challenges faced by schools and the potential solutions to those challenges. I passionately believe that every child has the right to a high-quality education and that we all have a part to play in achieving this ideal.

NOTES

NOTES

NOTES

Printed in Great Britain
by Amazon

35829554R00098